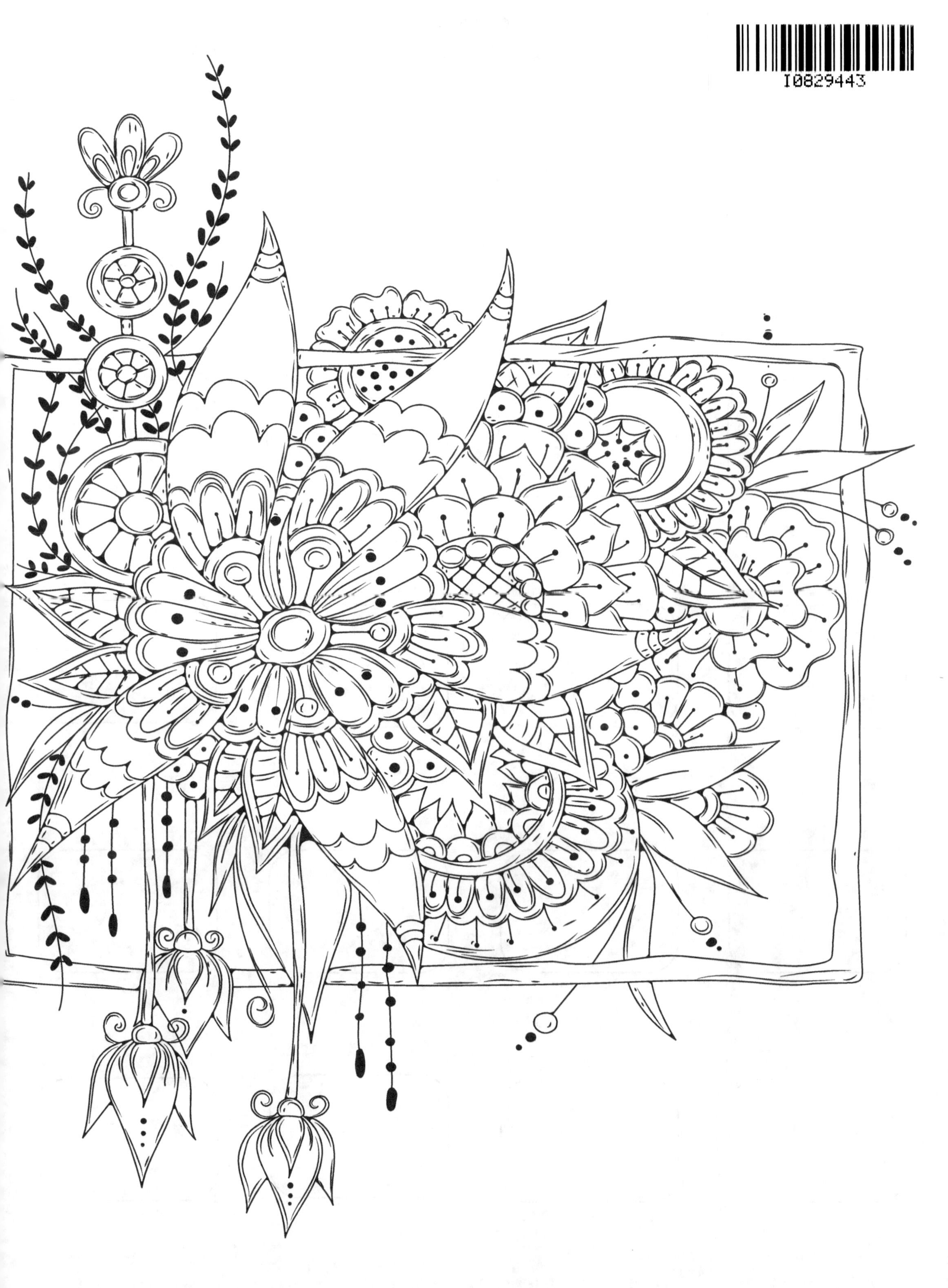

COLOR TEST PAGE

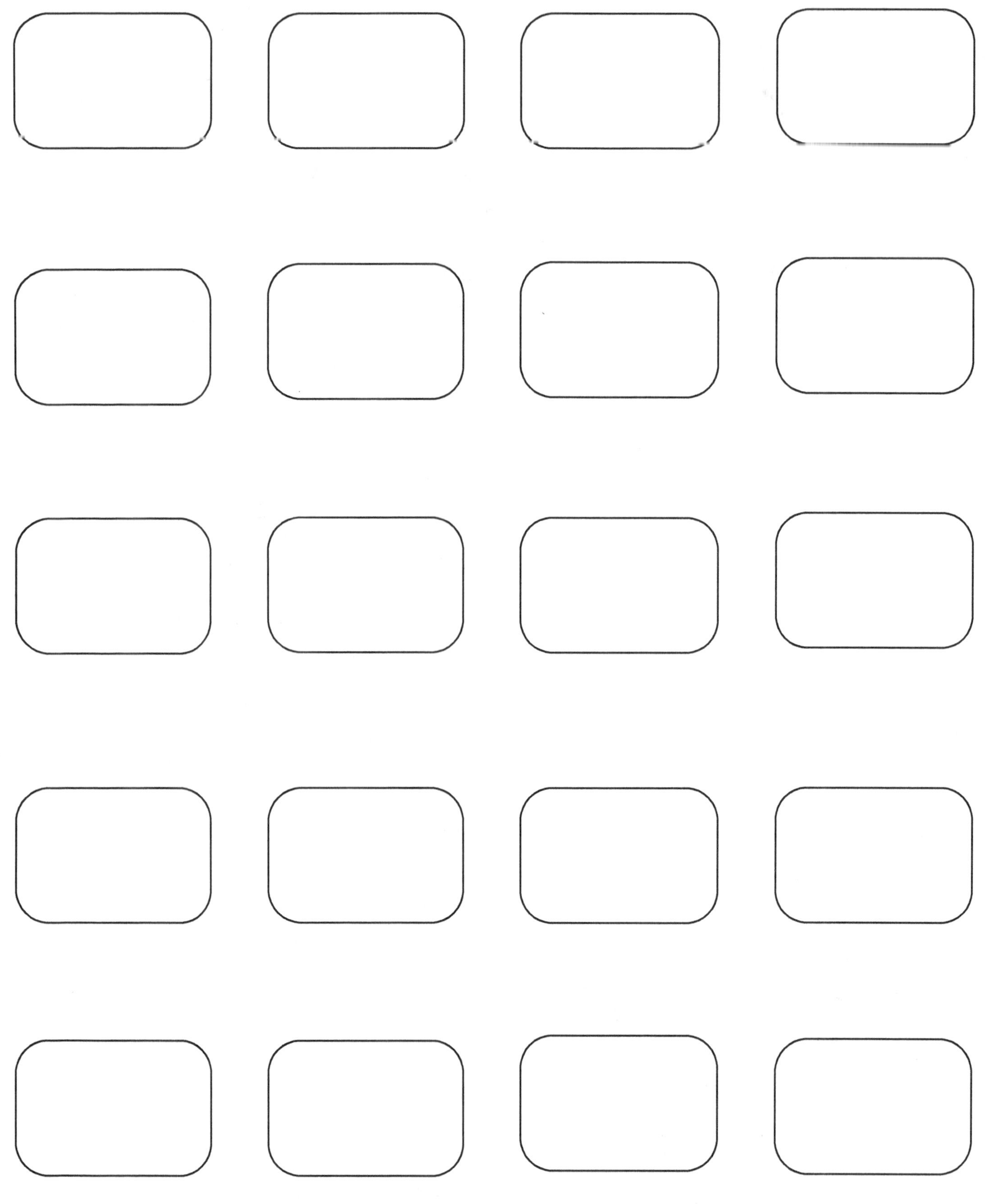

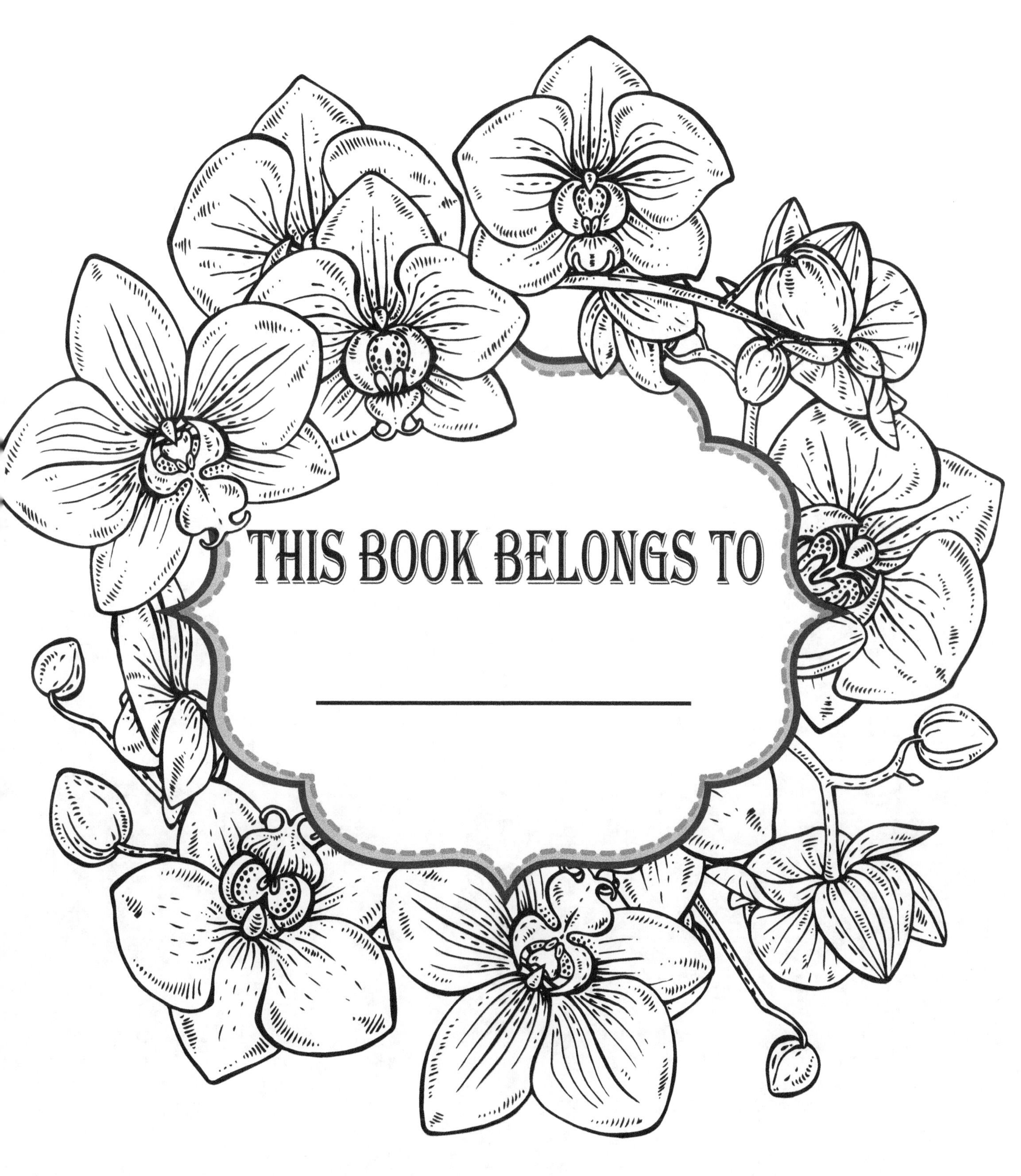
THIS BOOK BELONGS TO

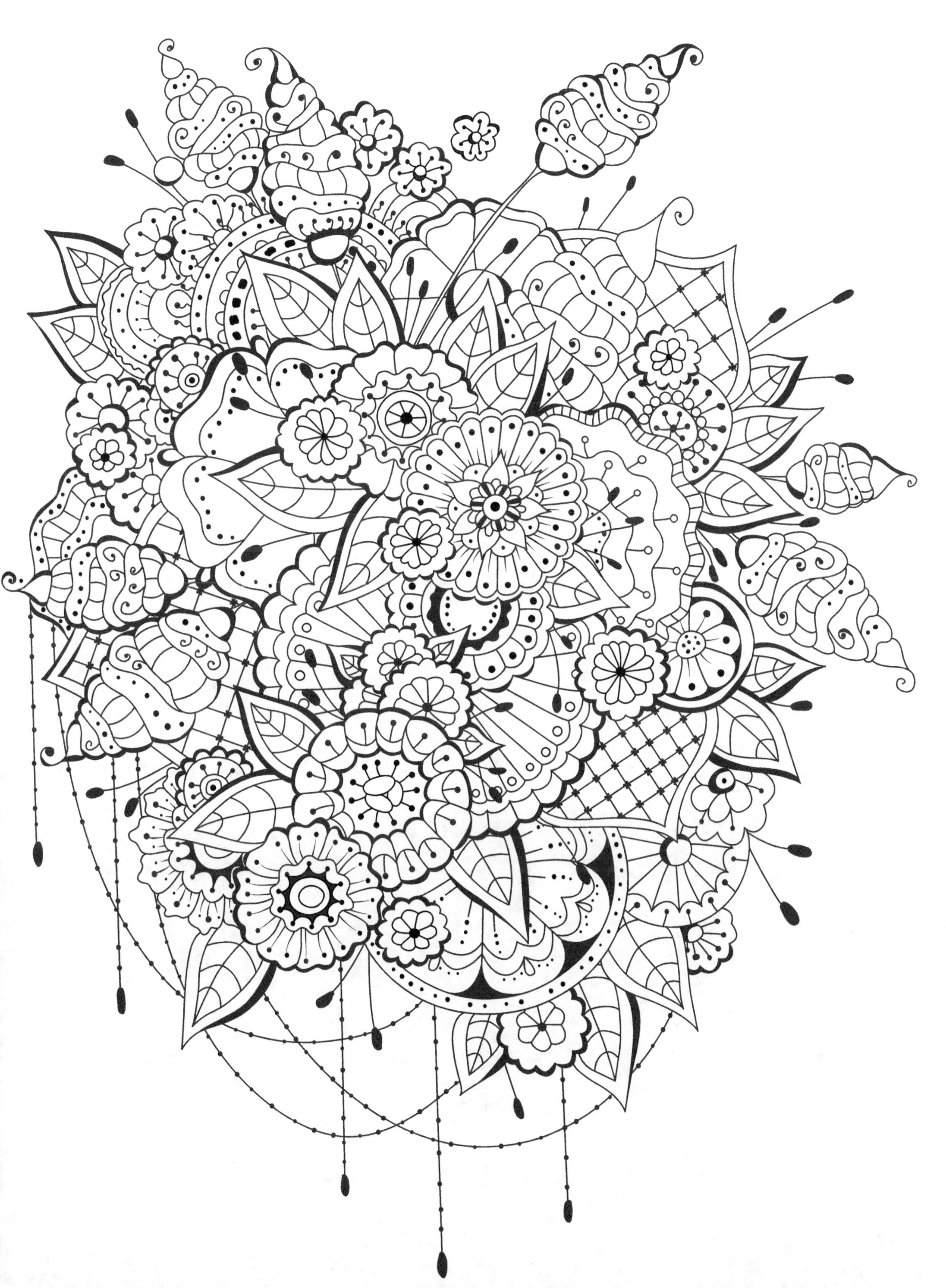

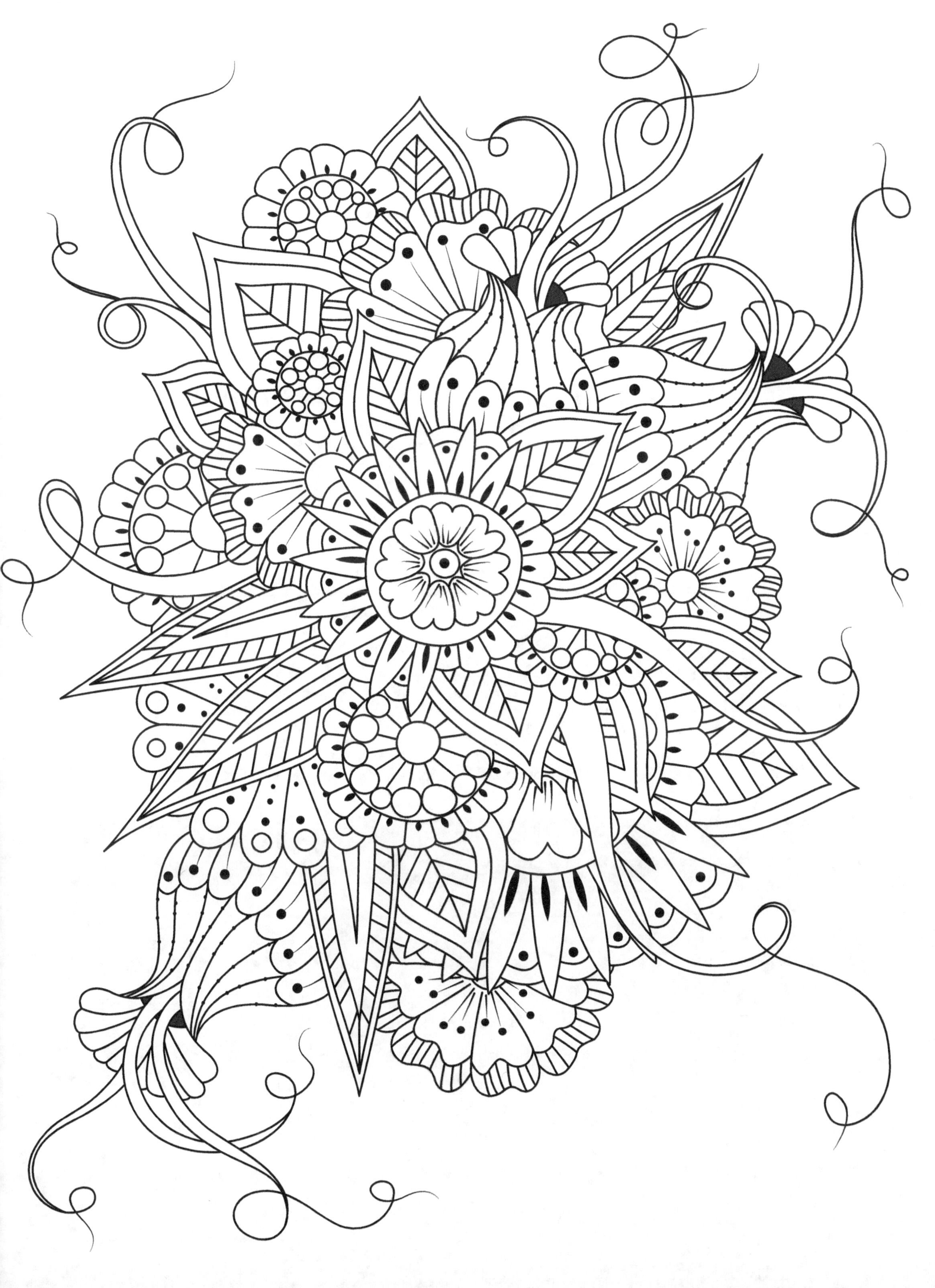

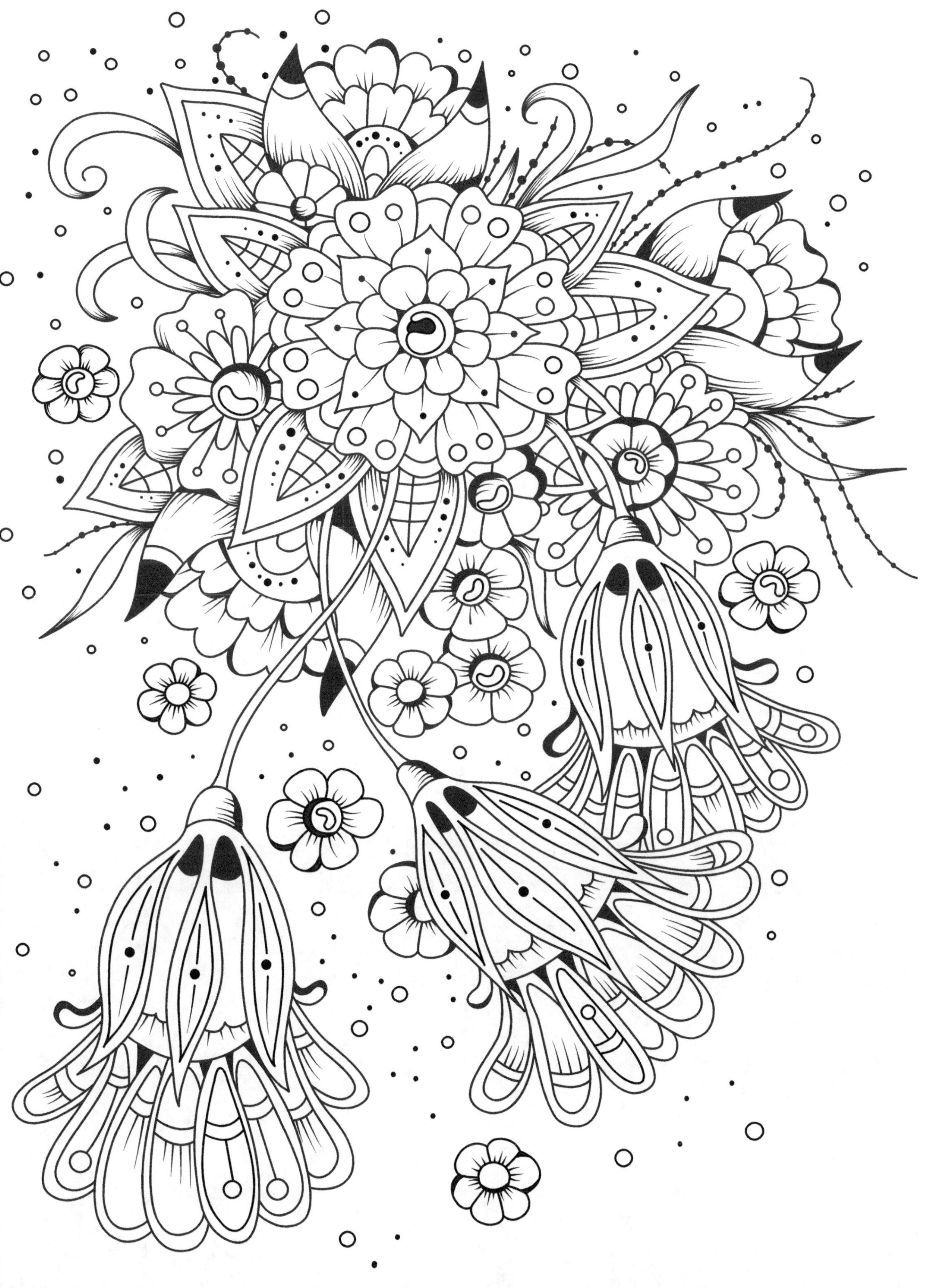

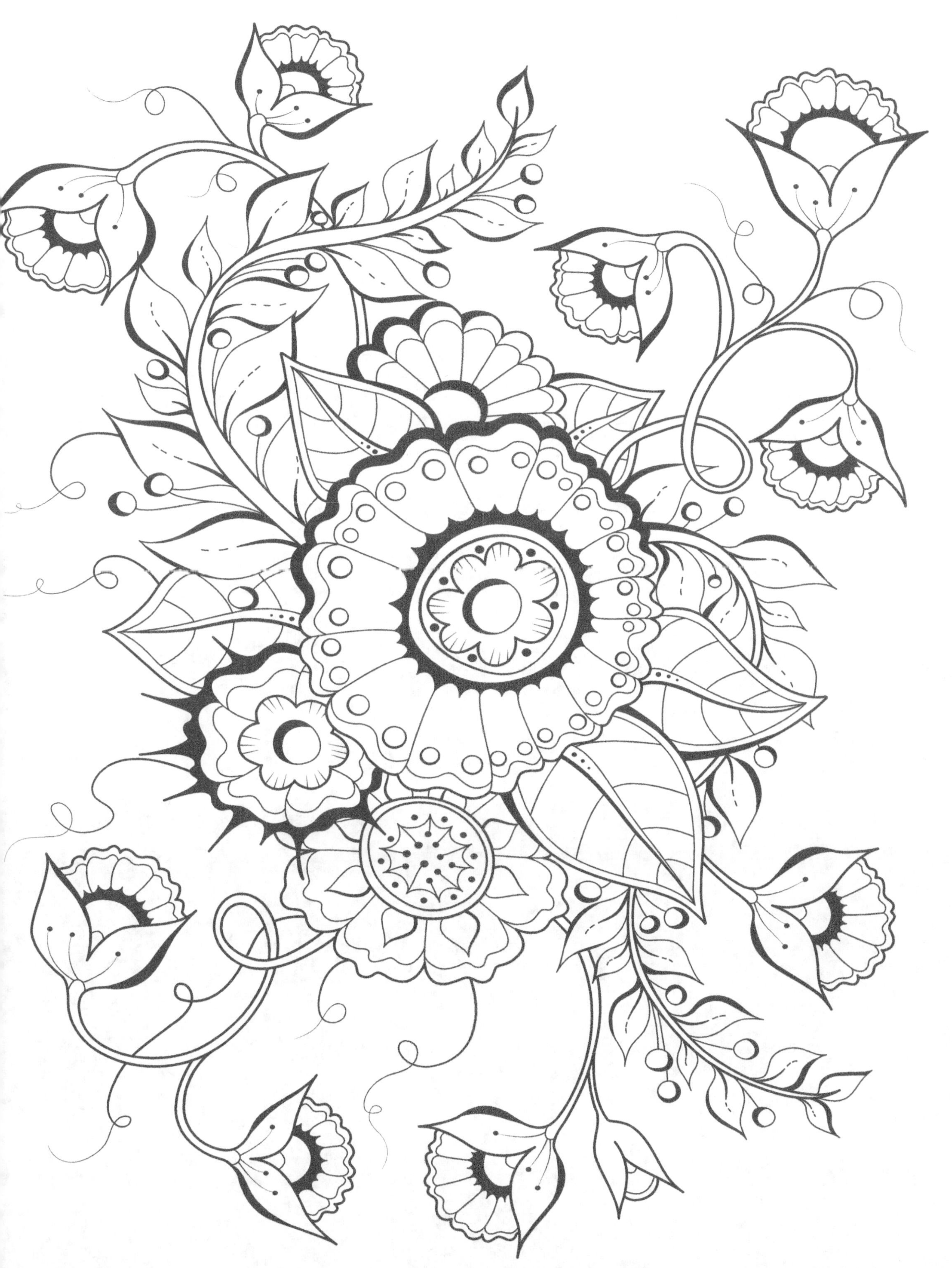

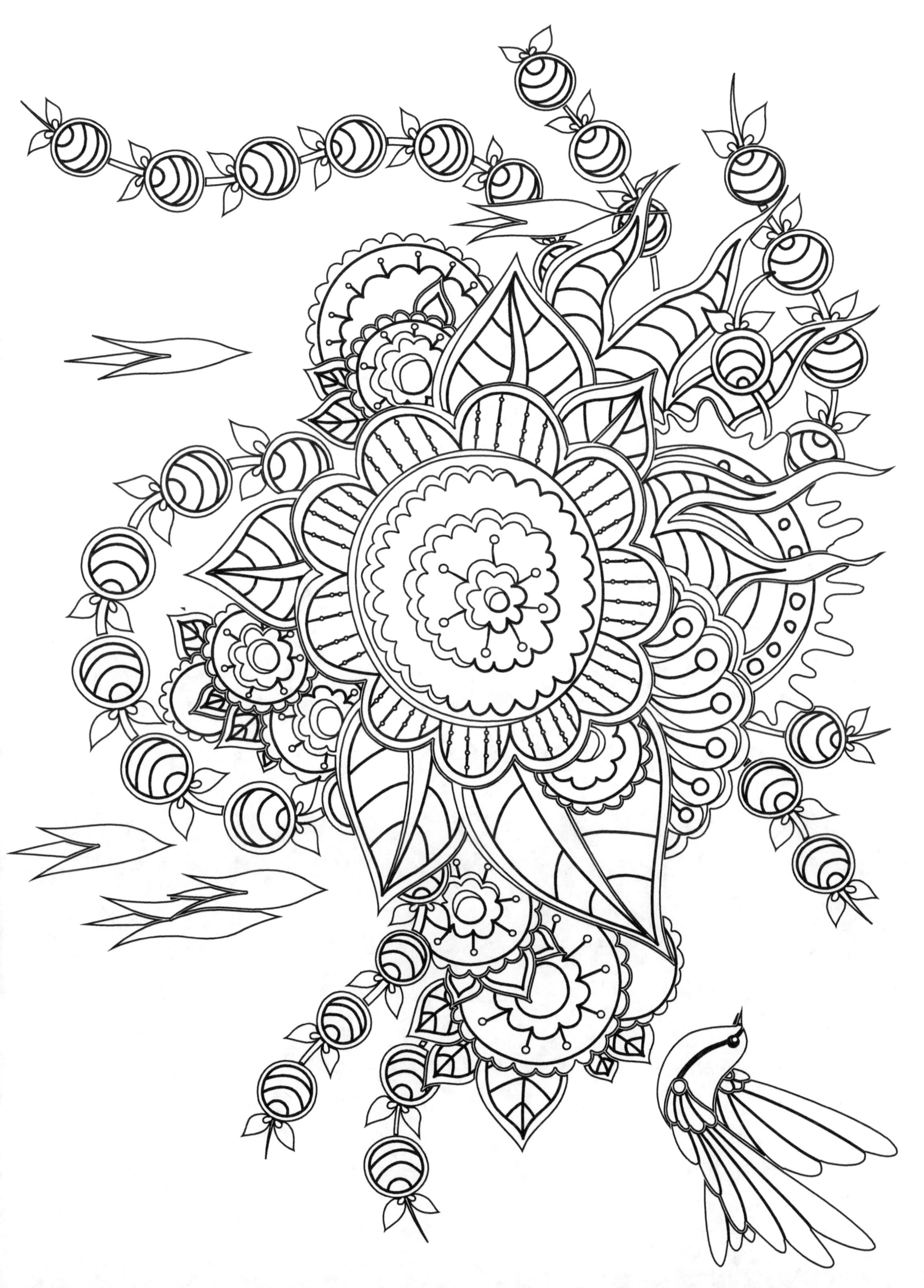

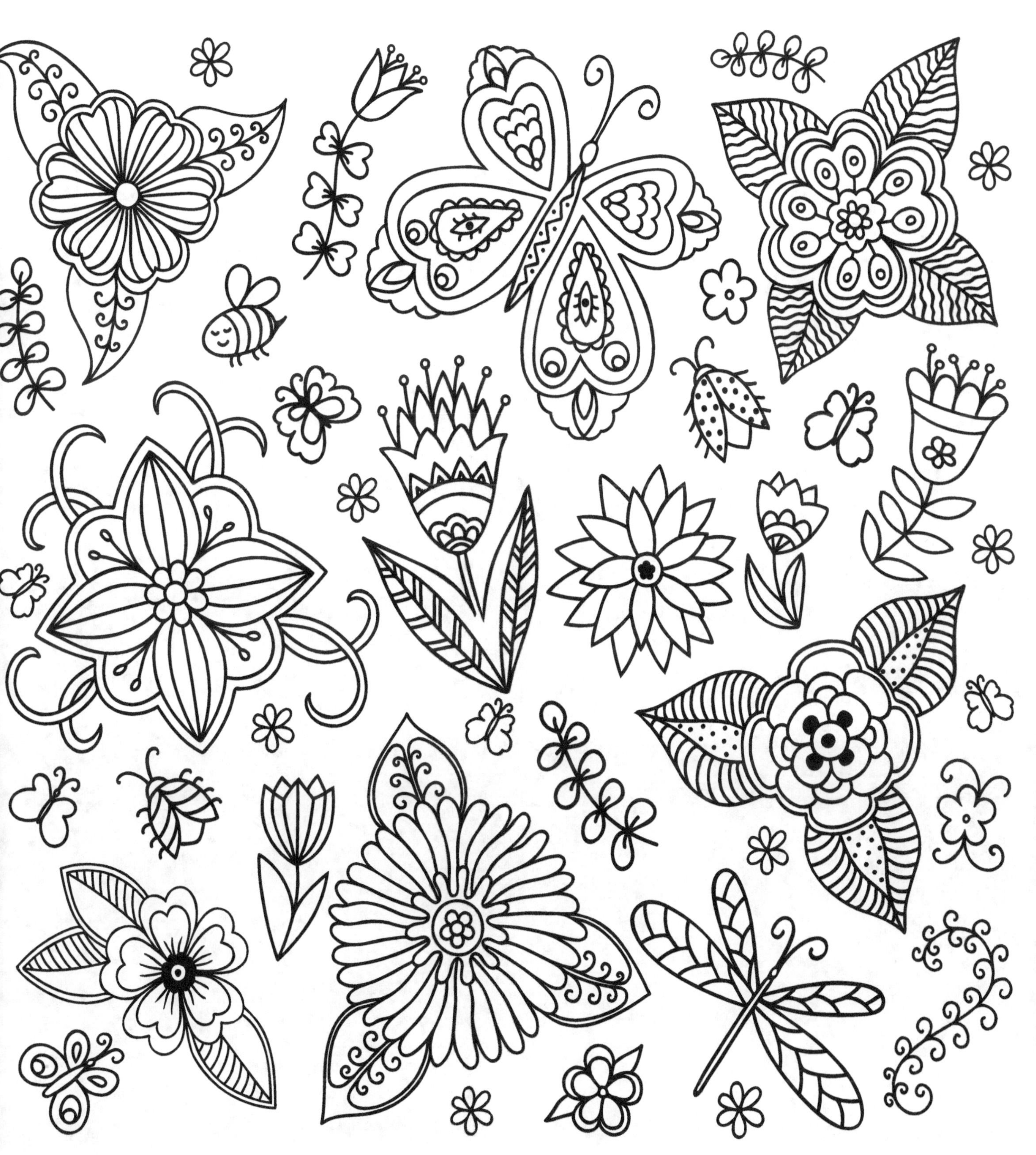

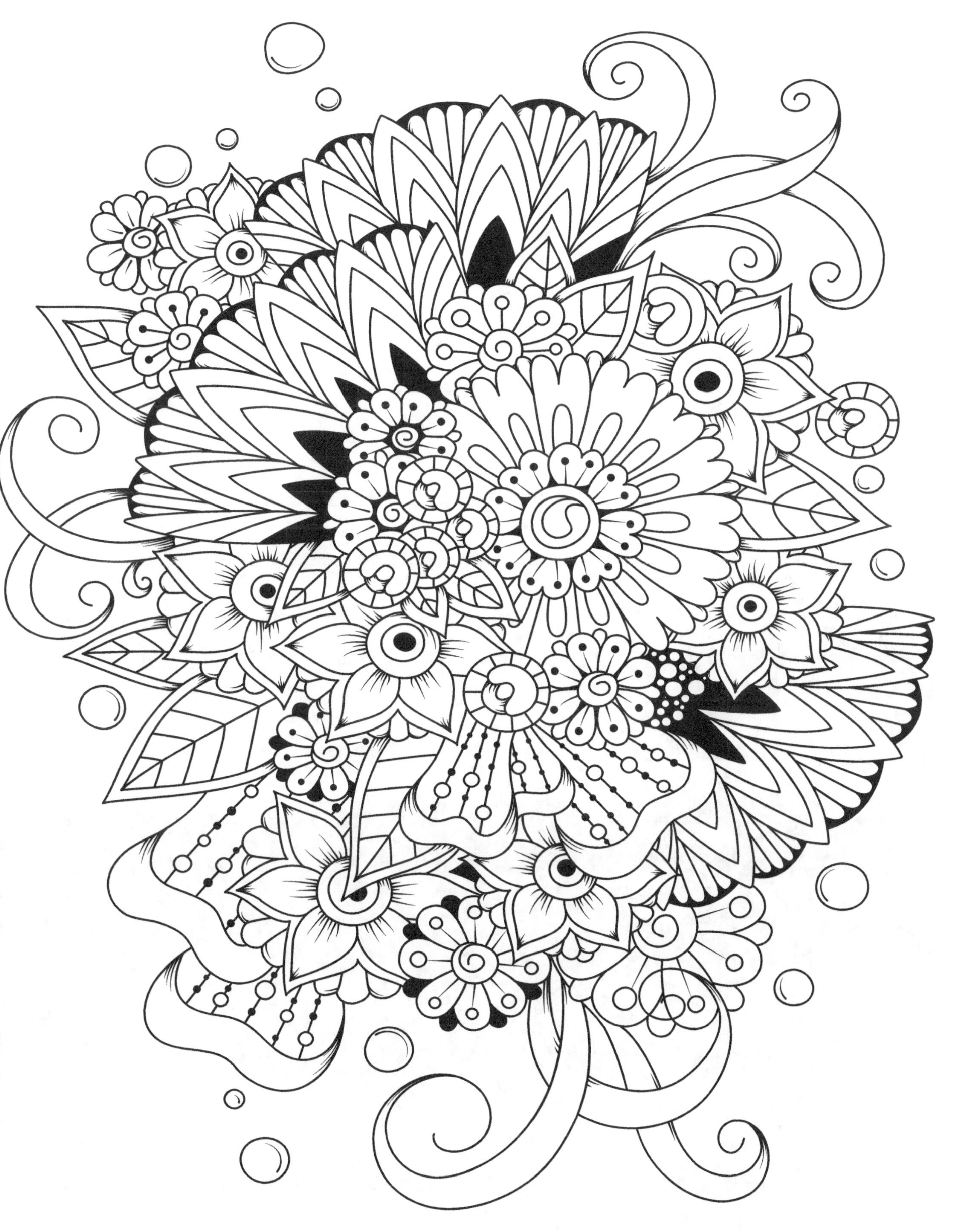

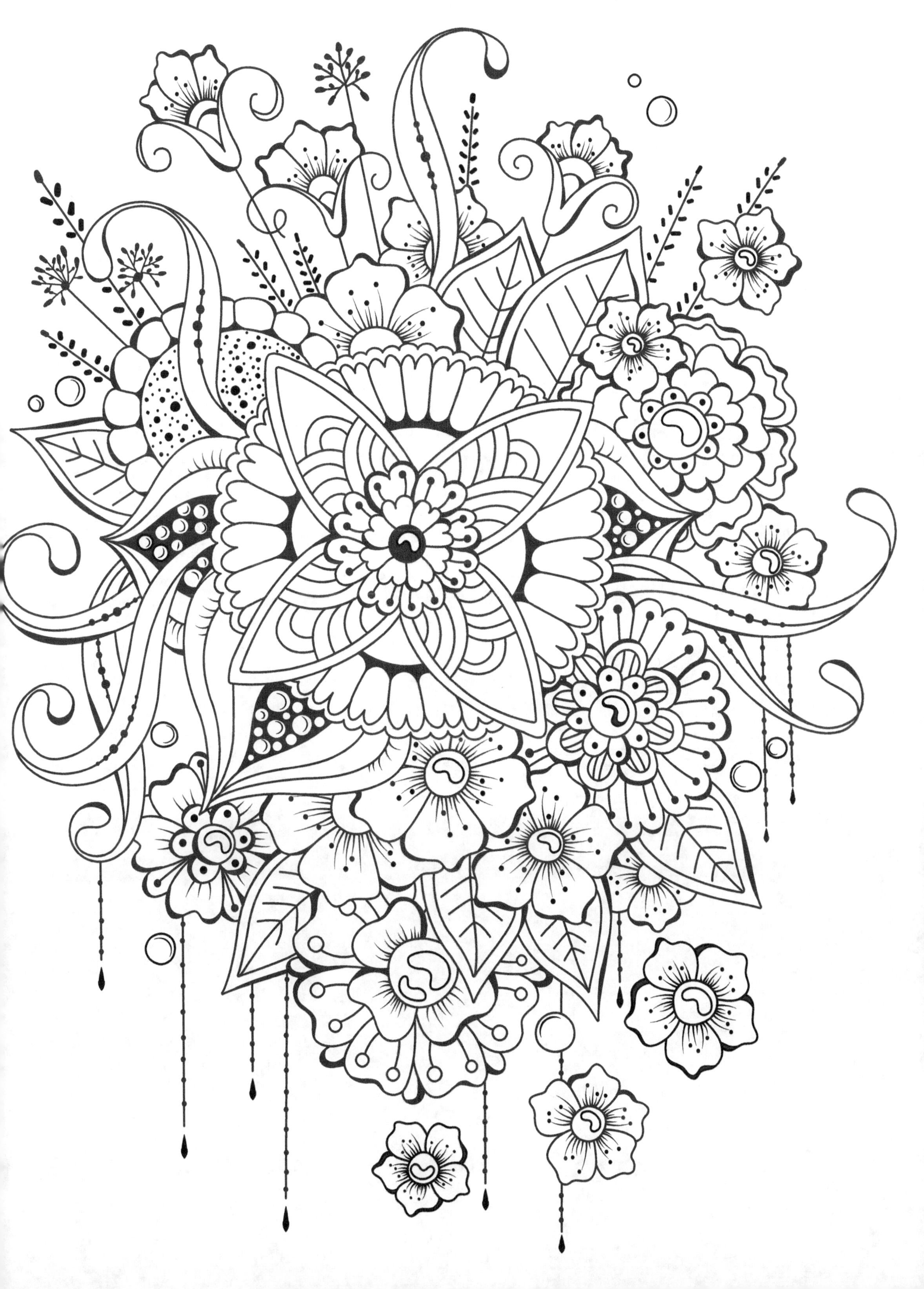

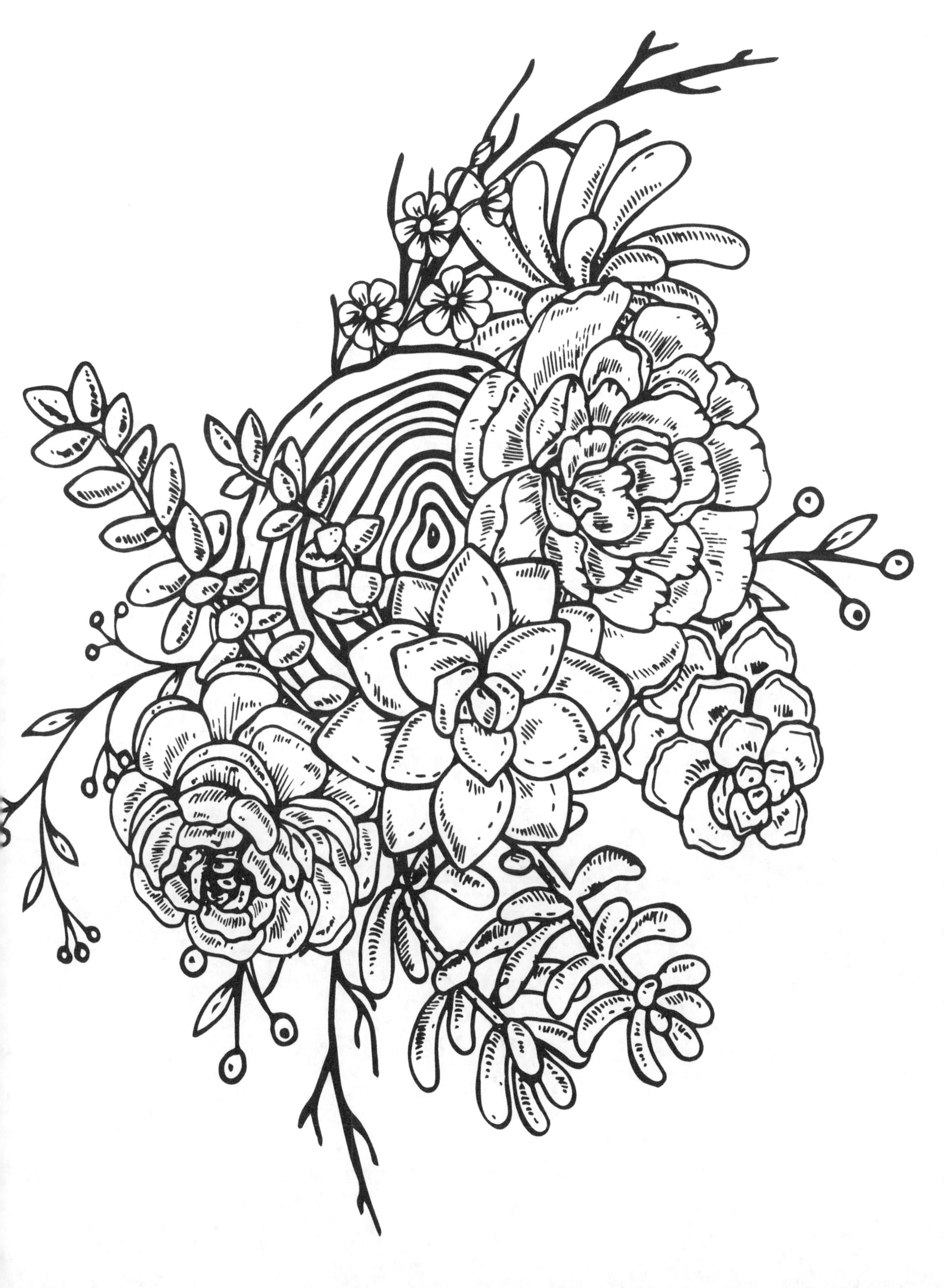

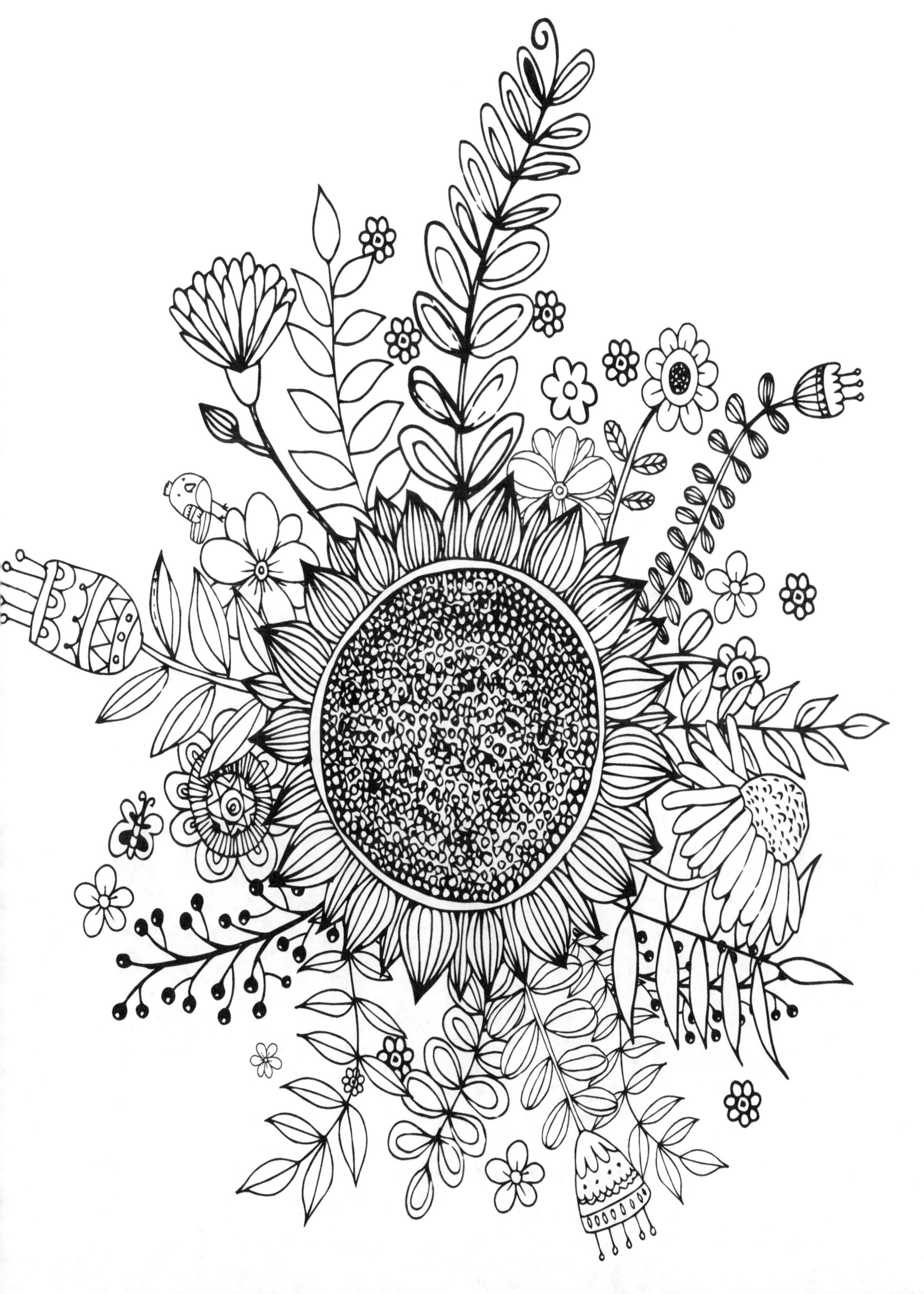

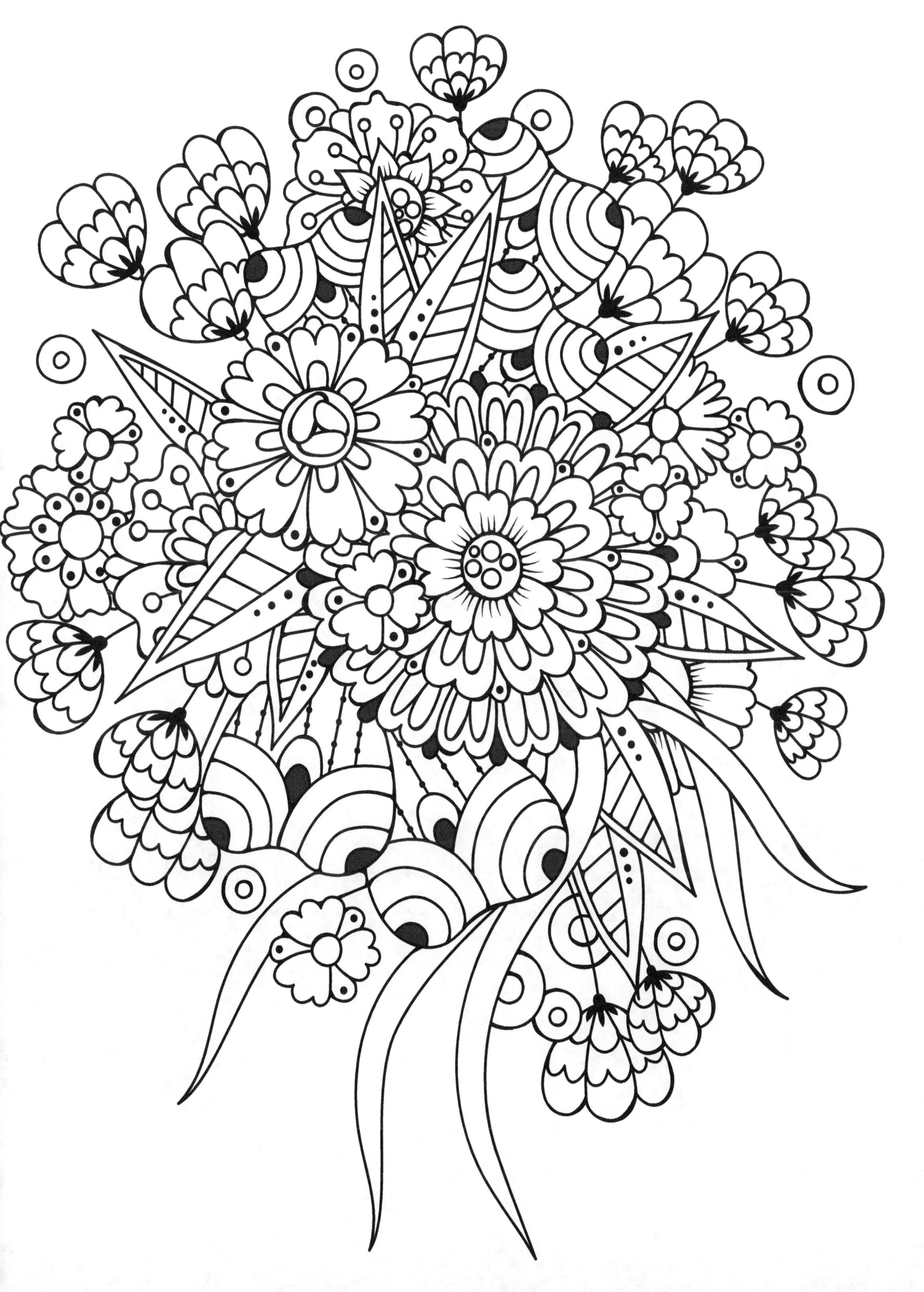

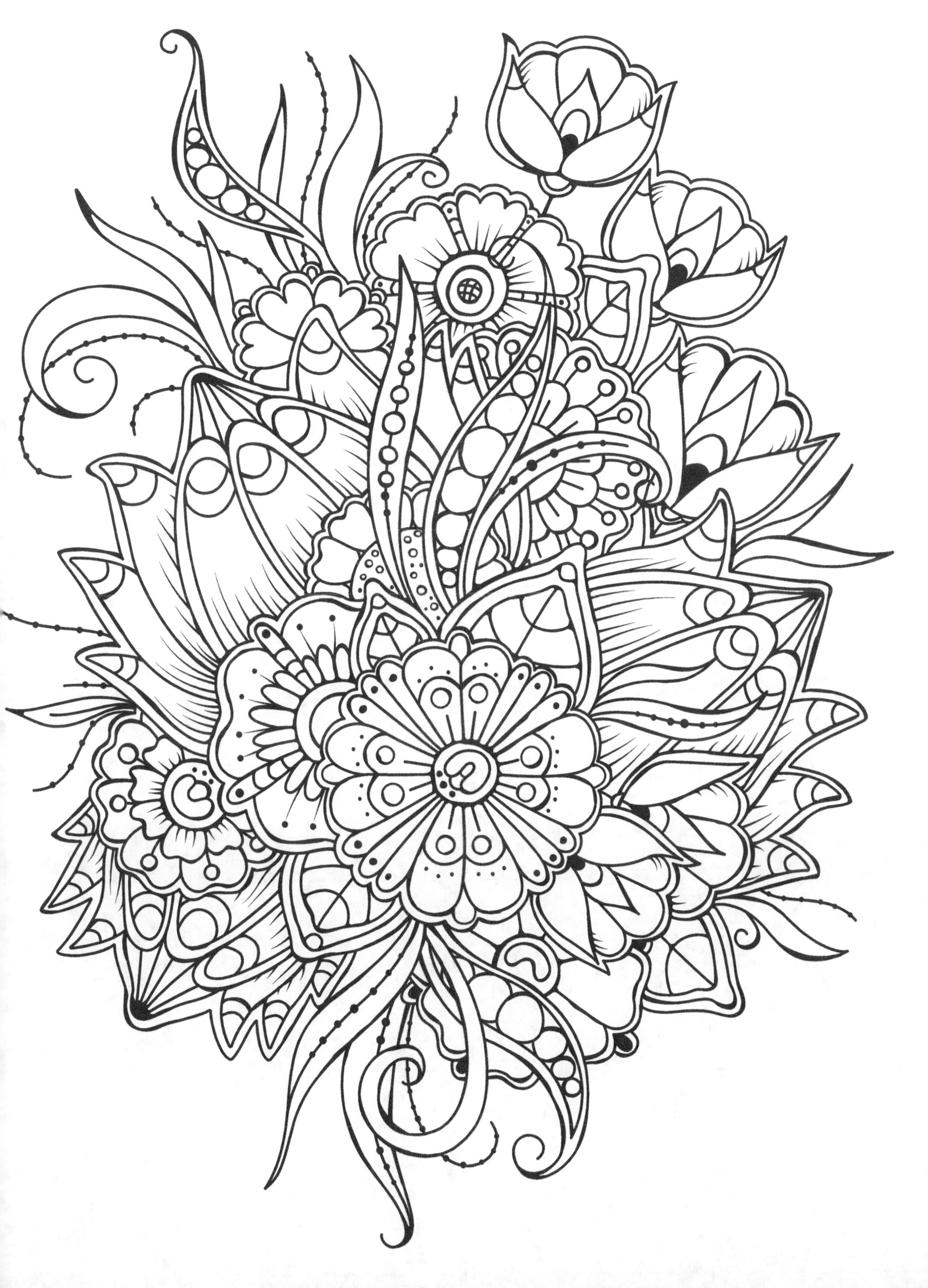

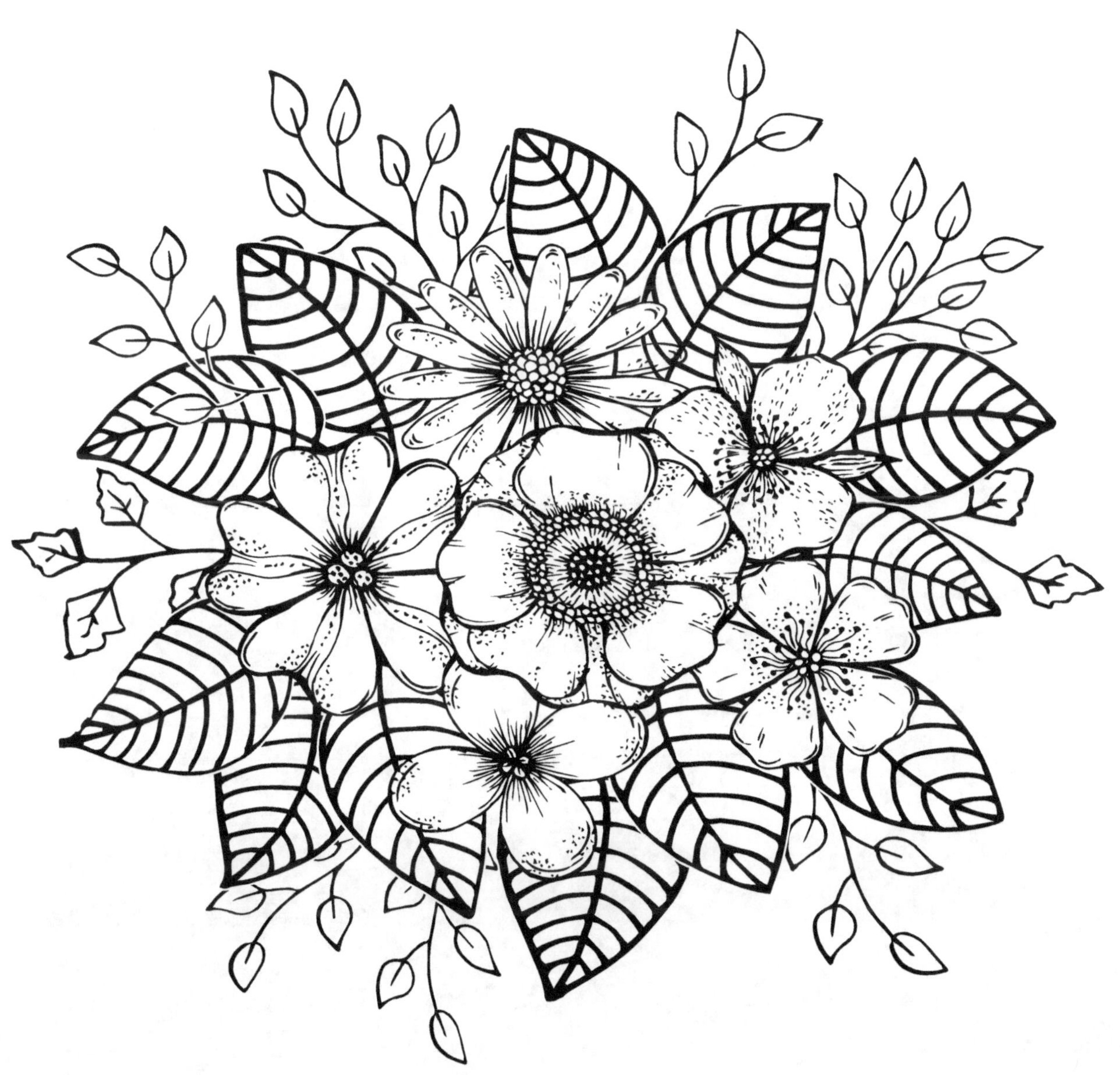

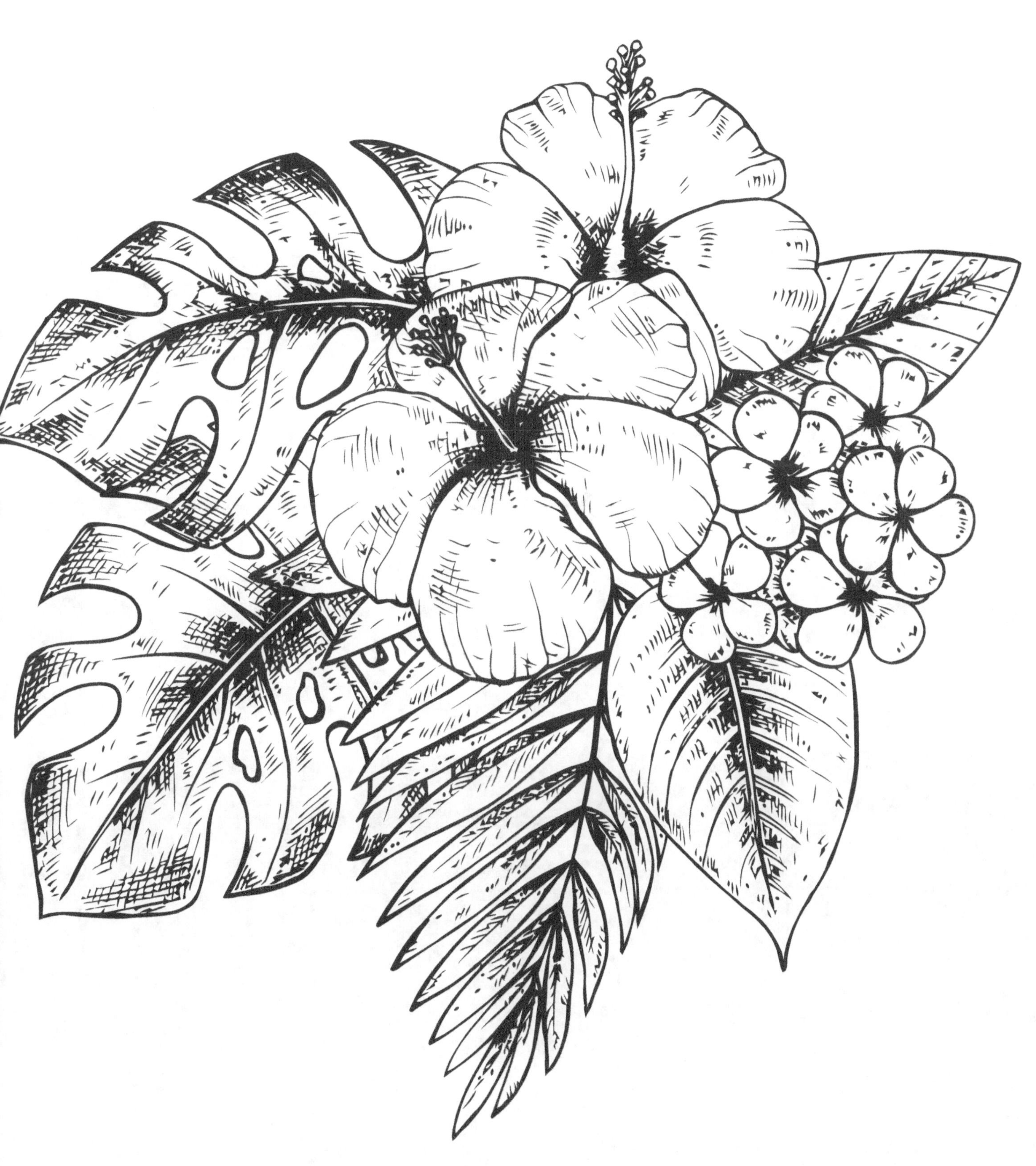

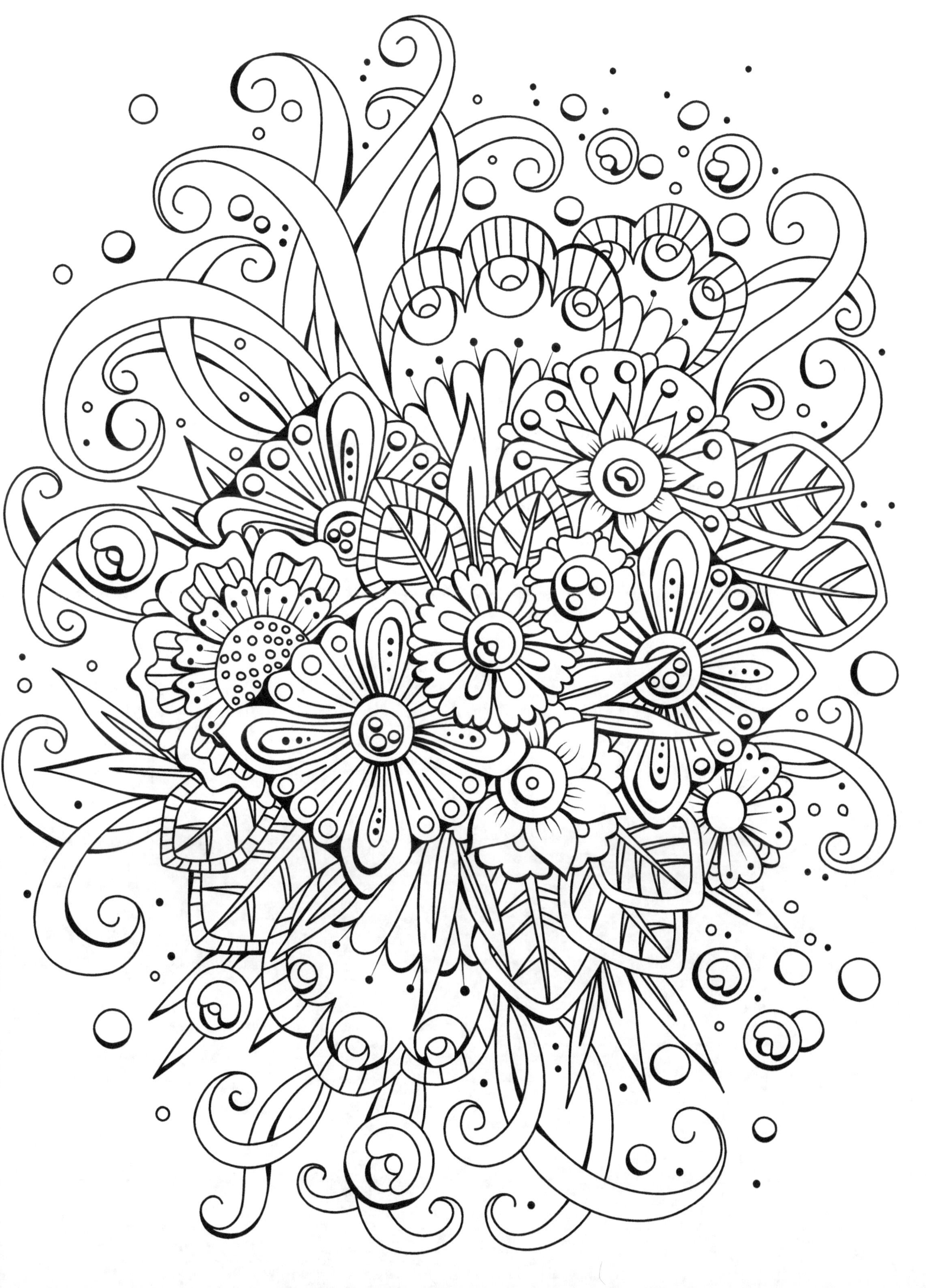

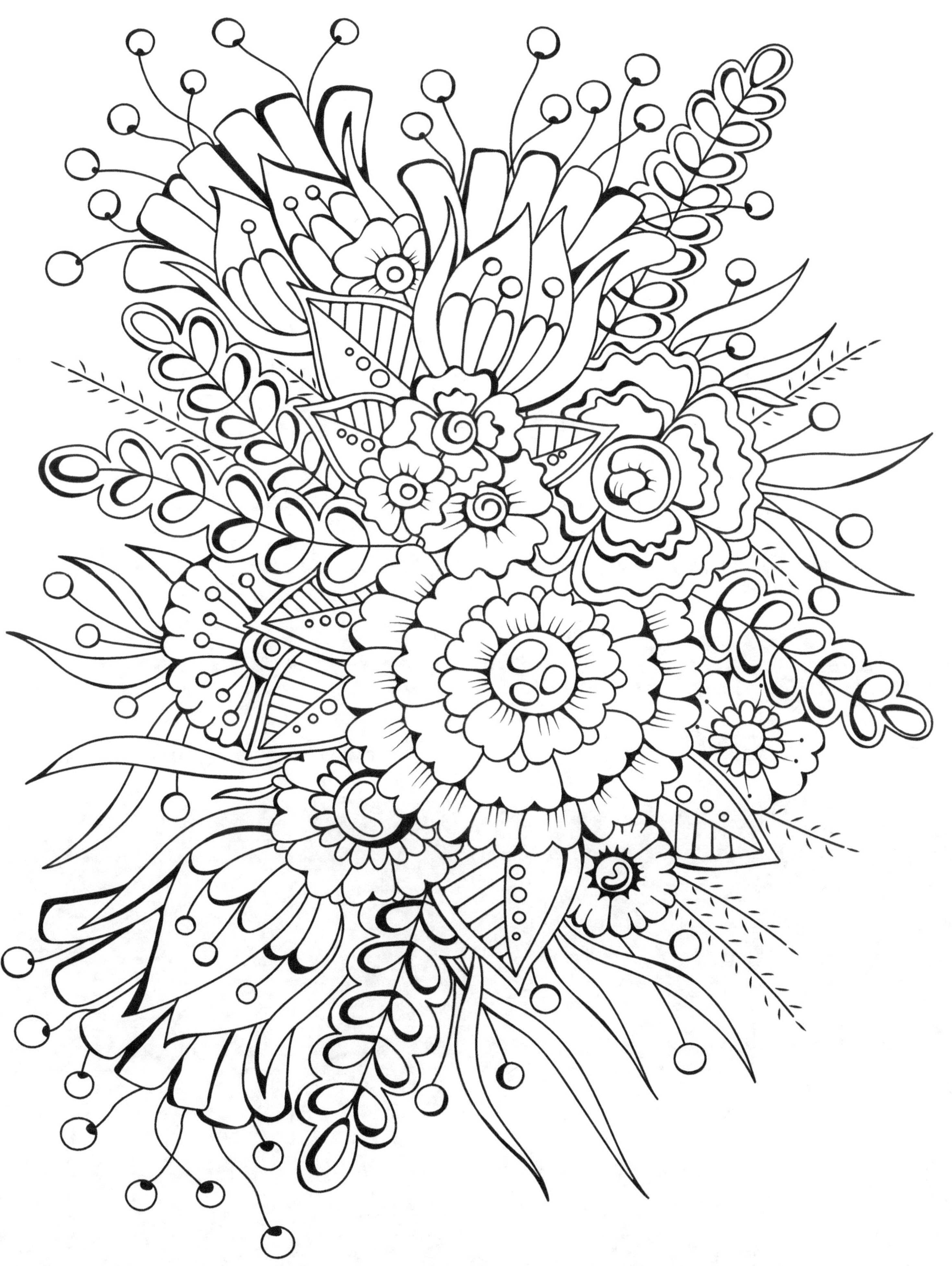

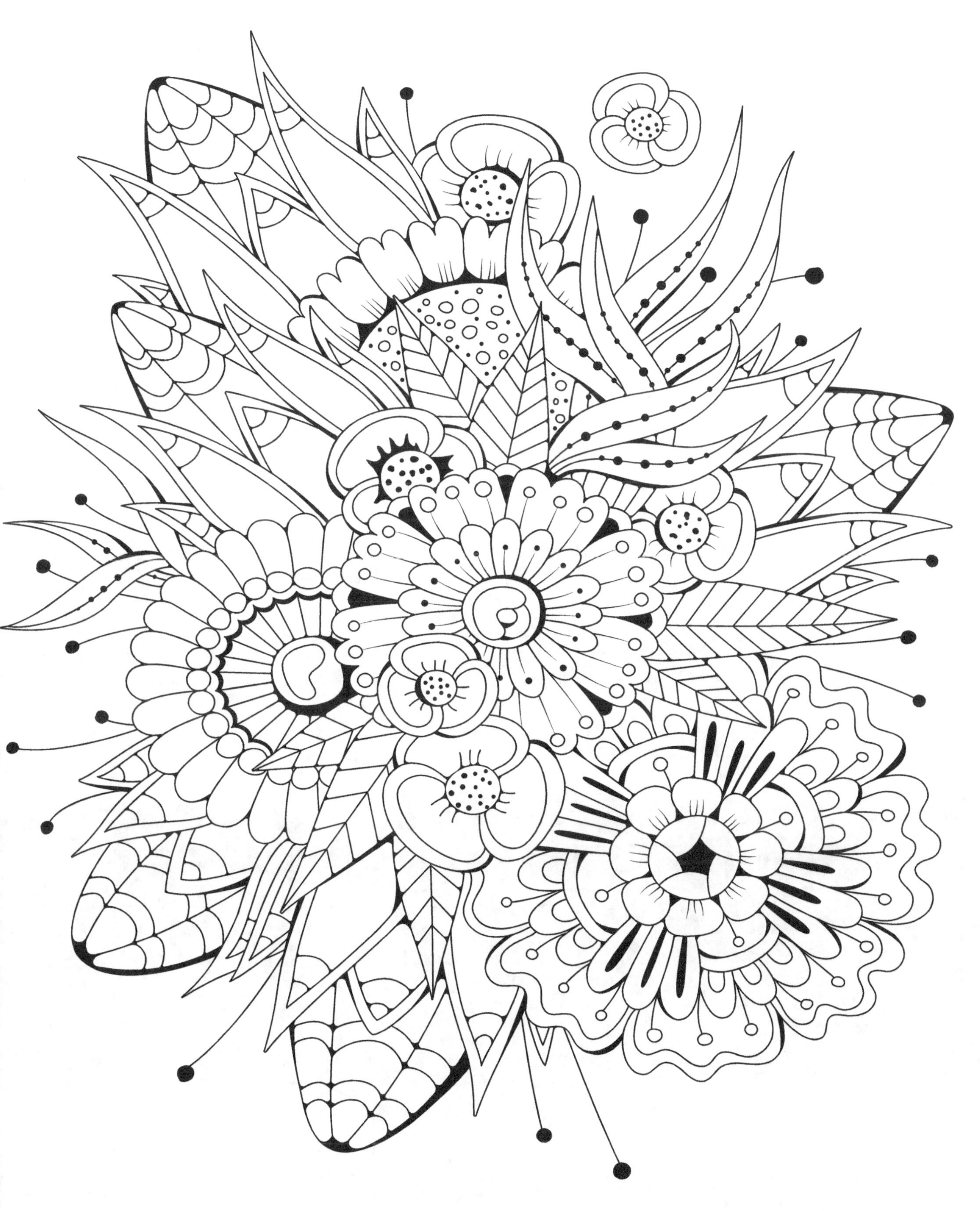

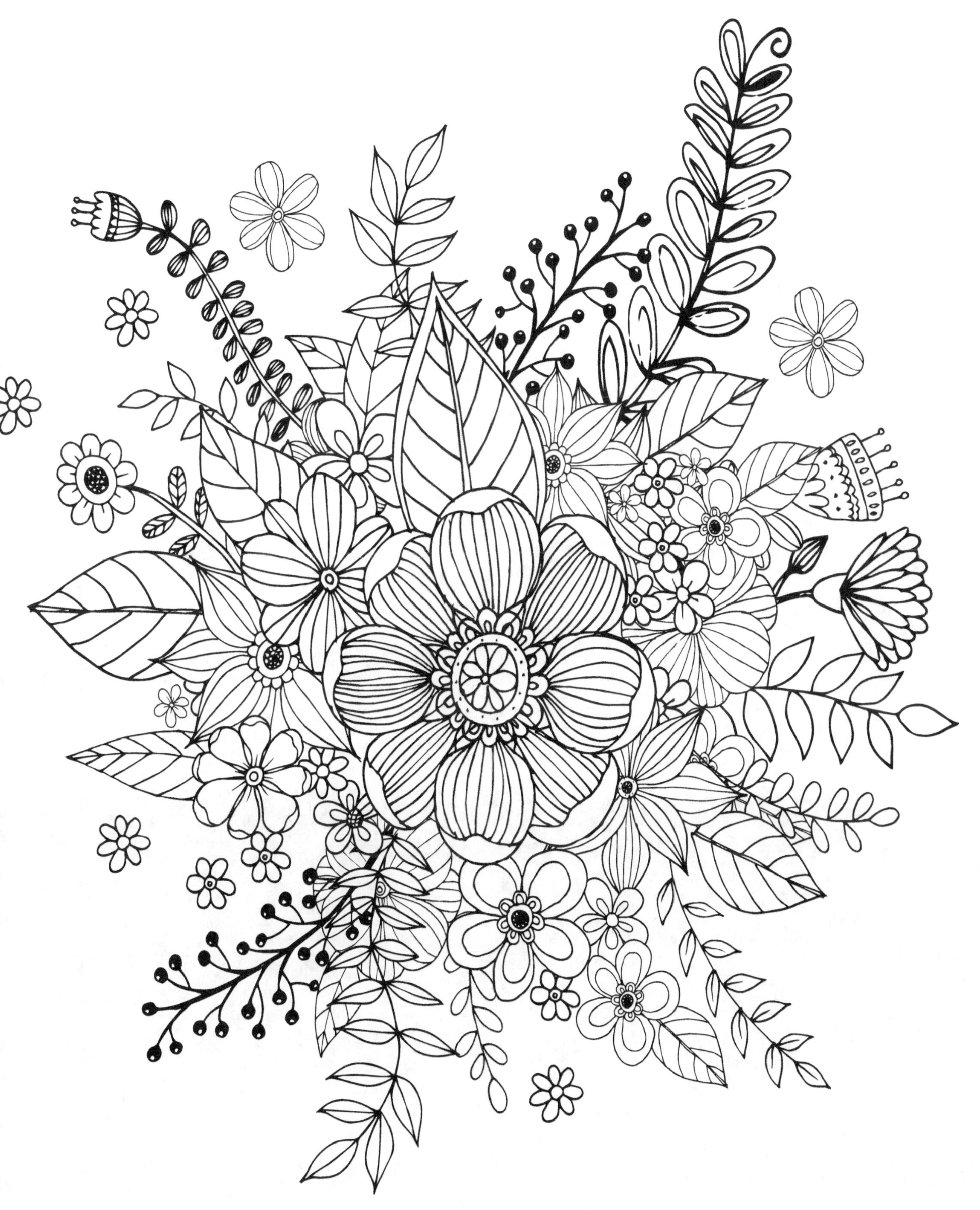

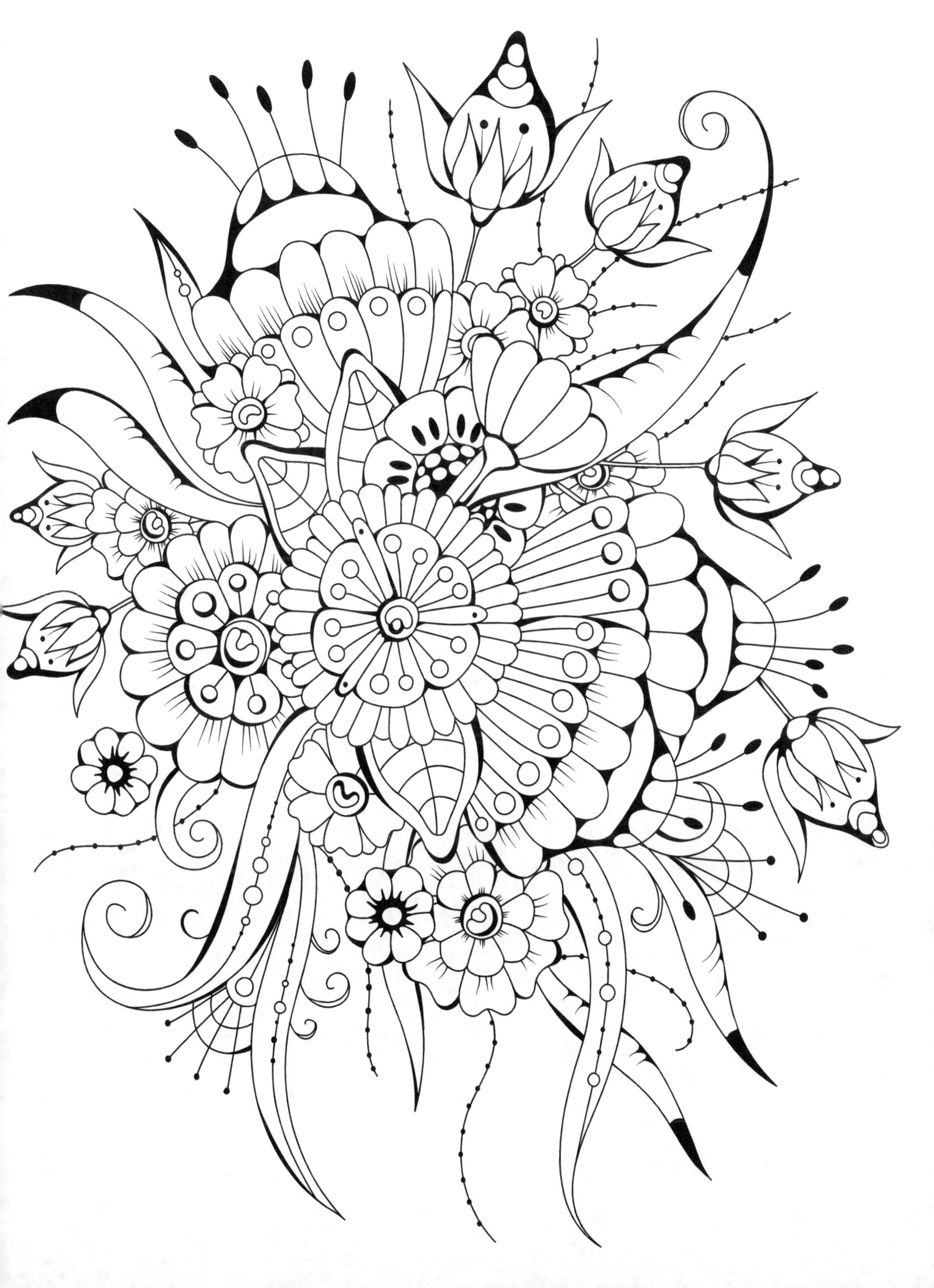

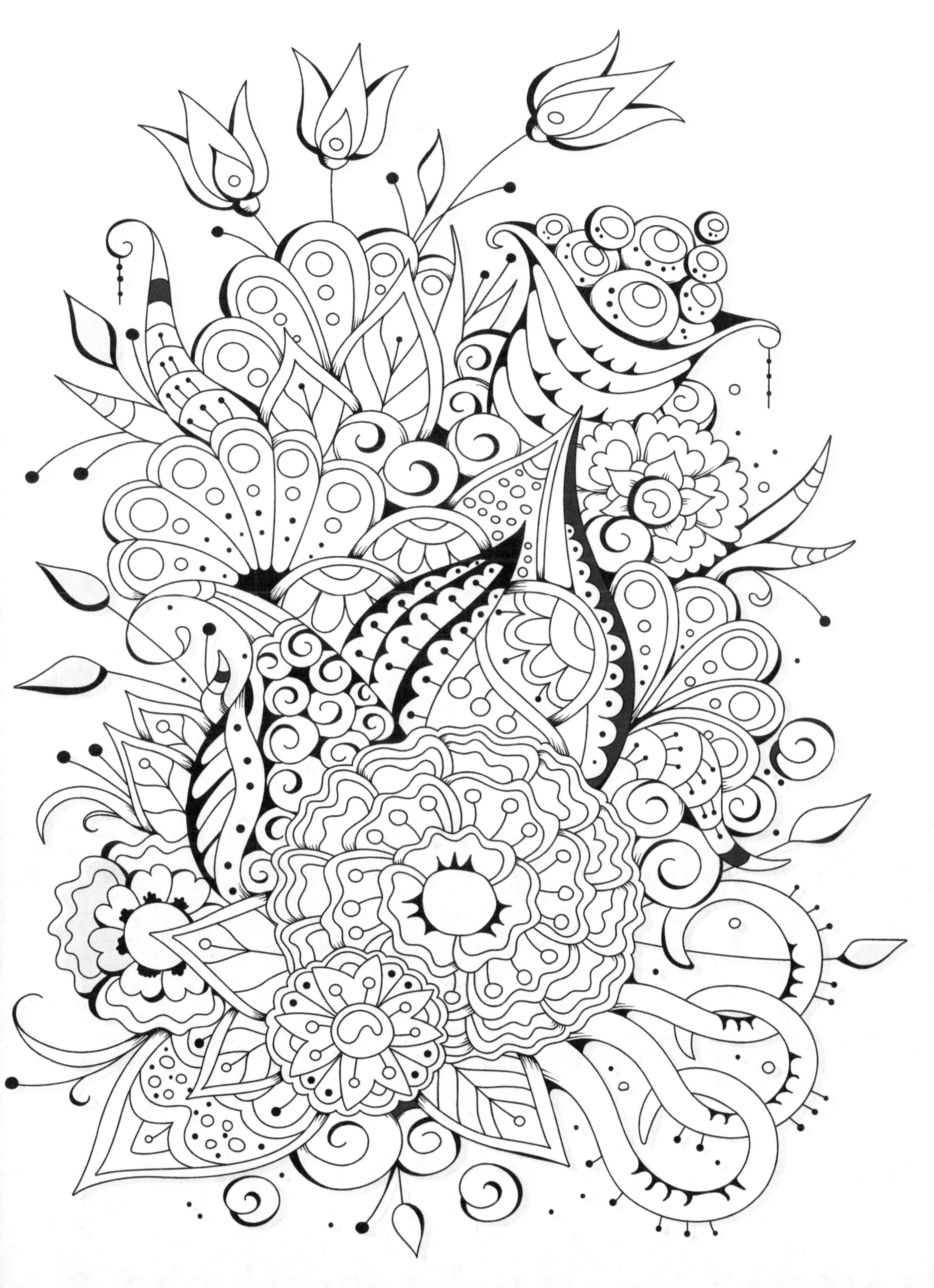

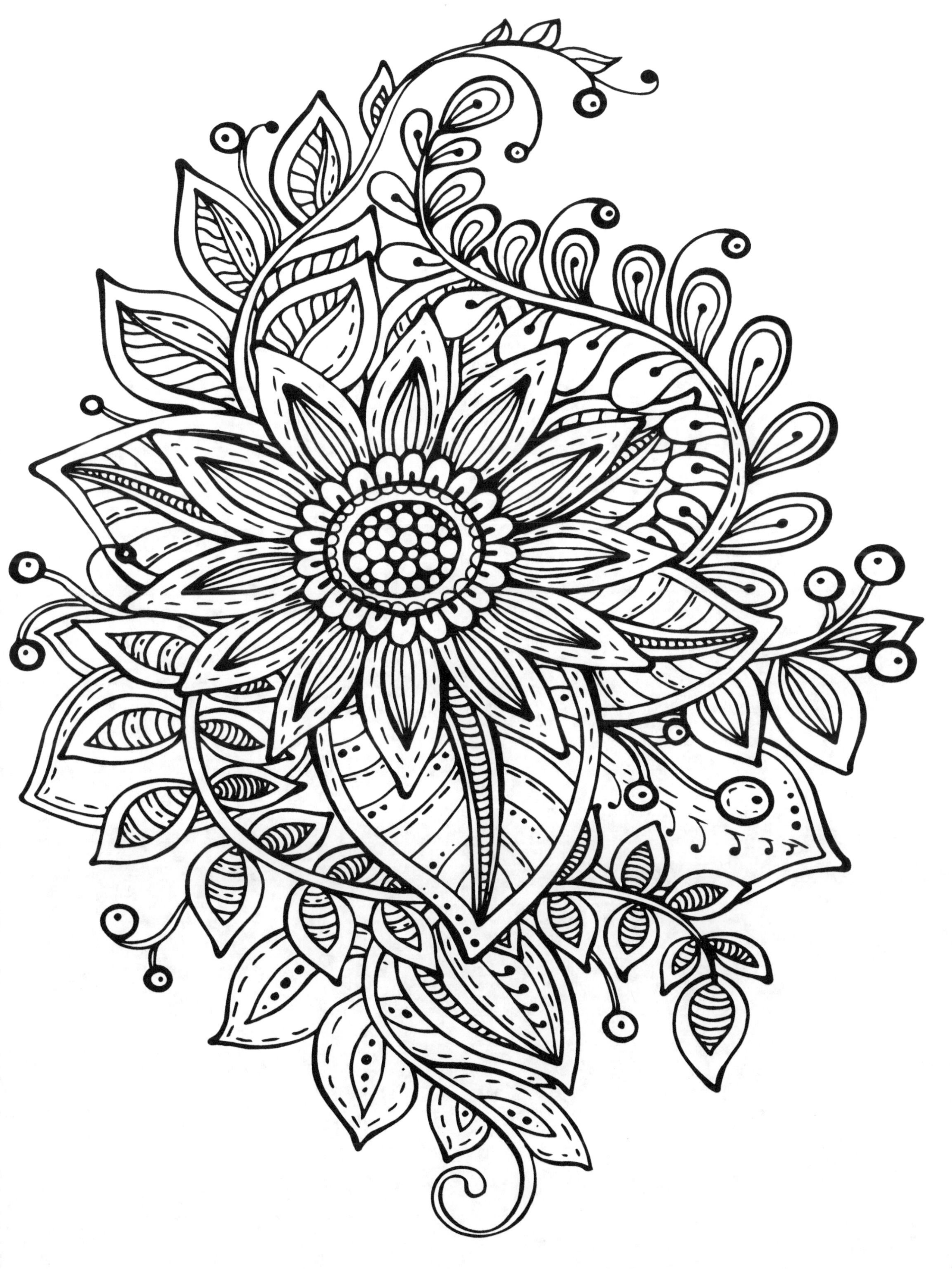

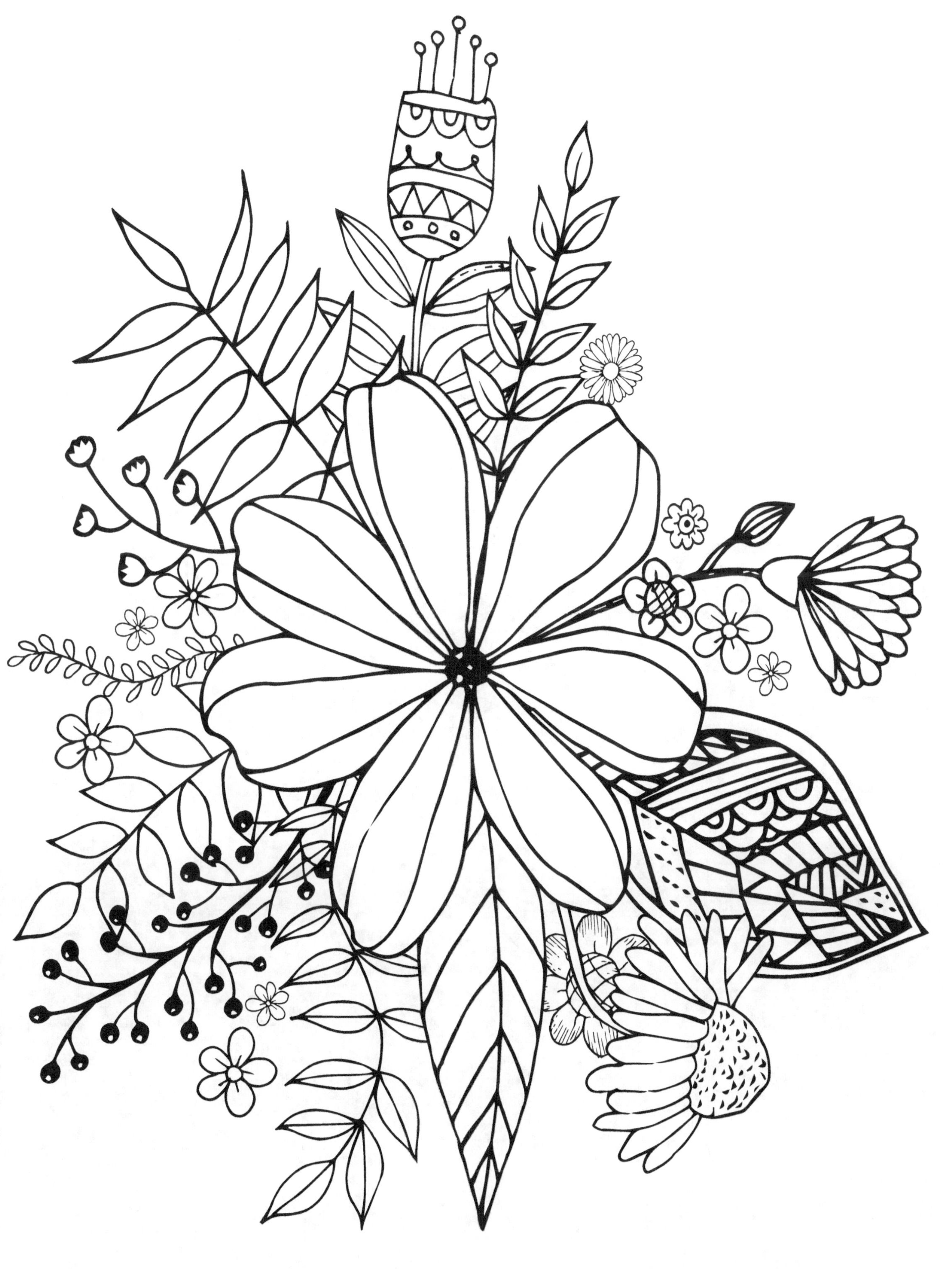

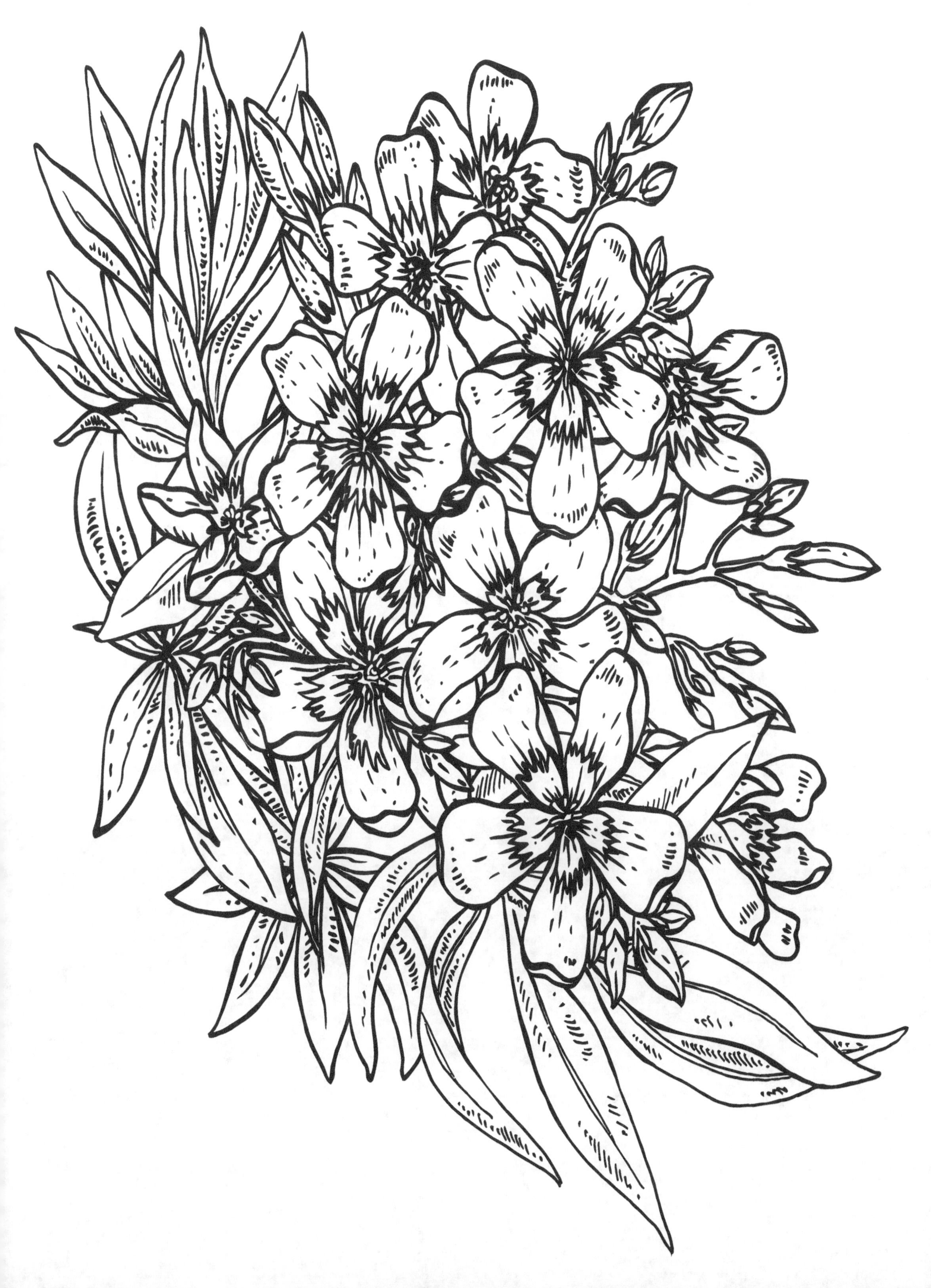

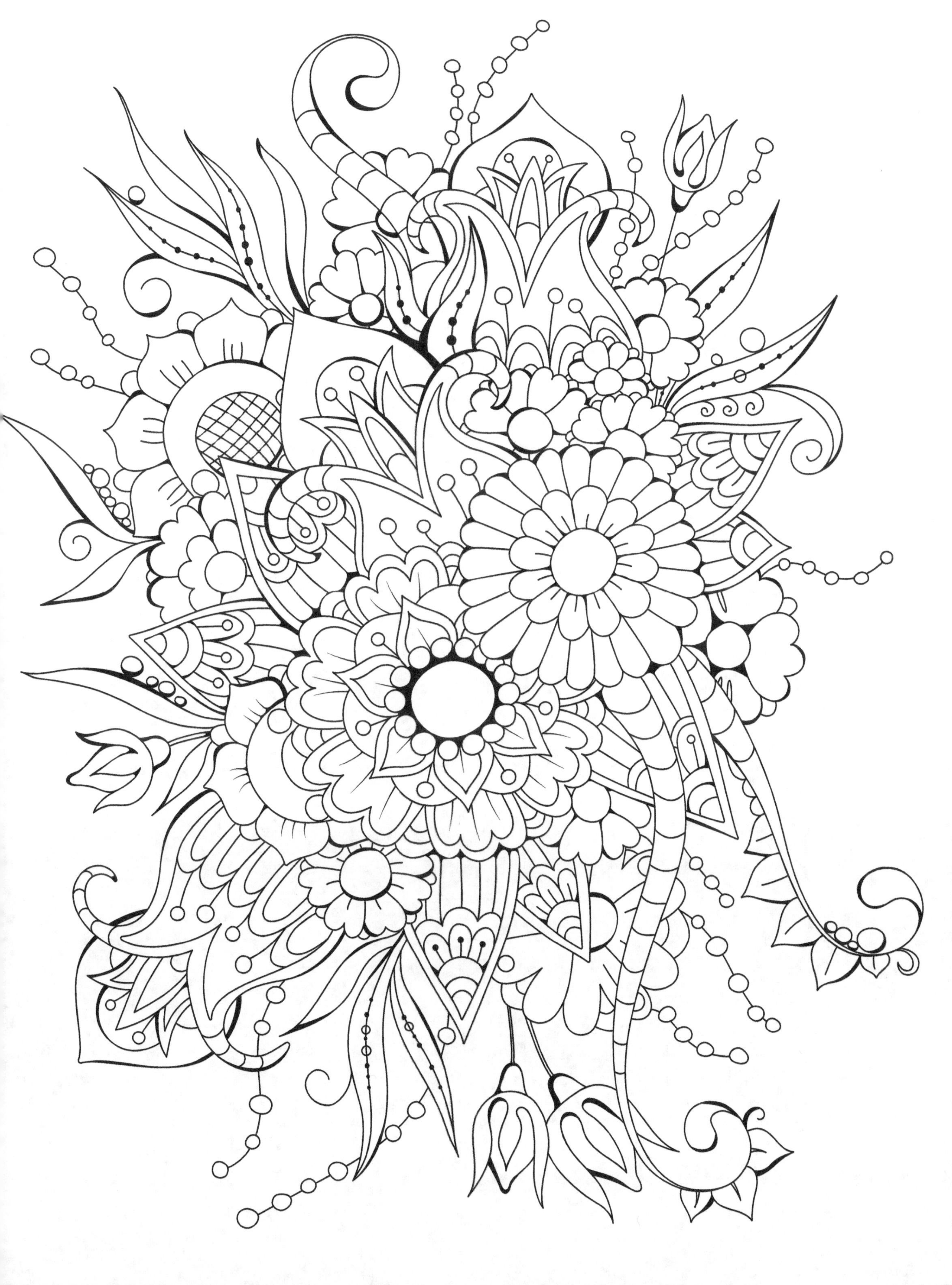

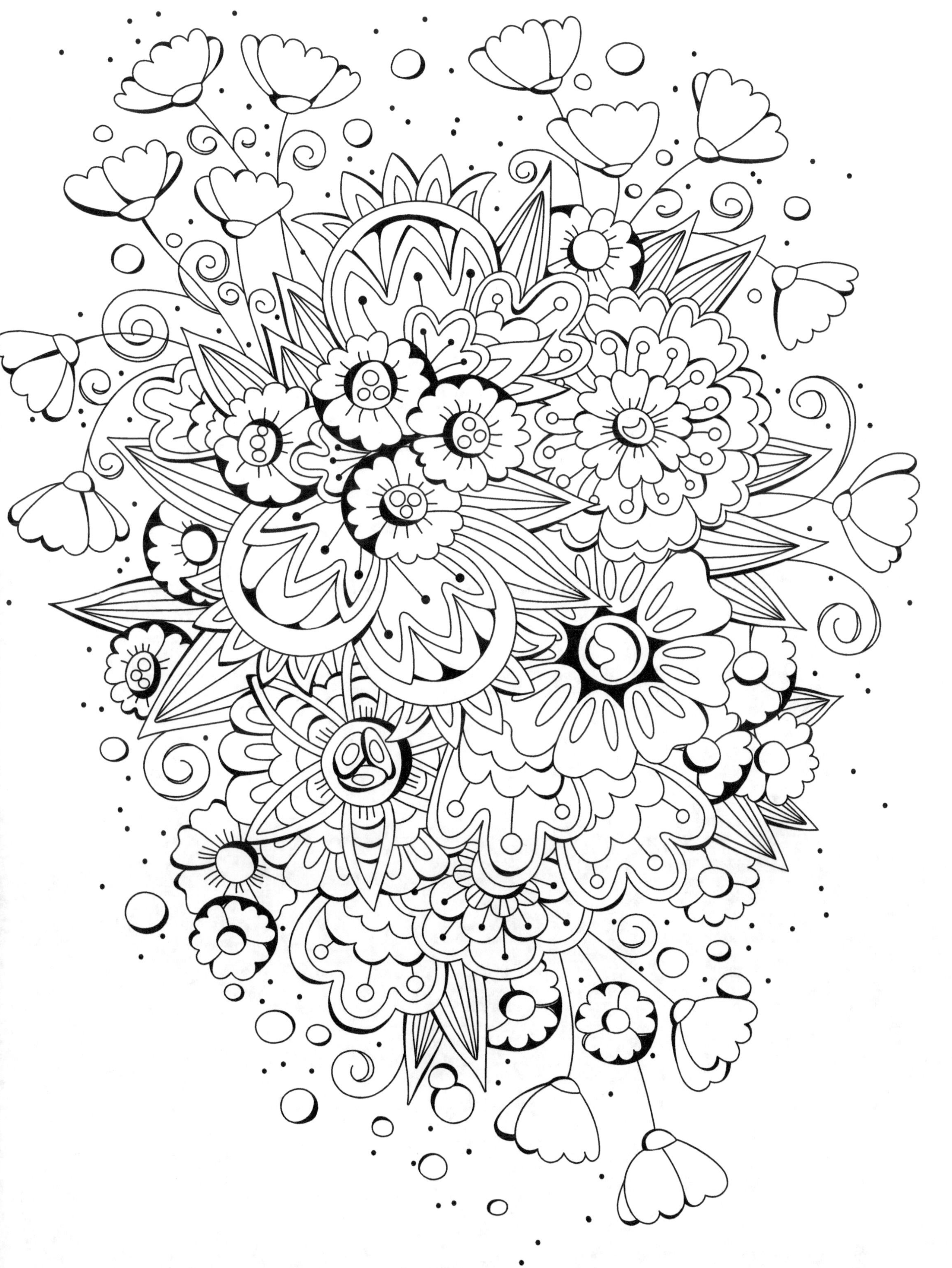

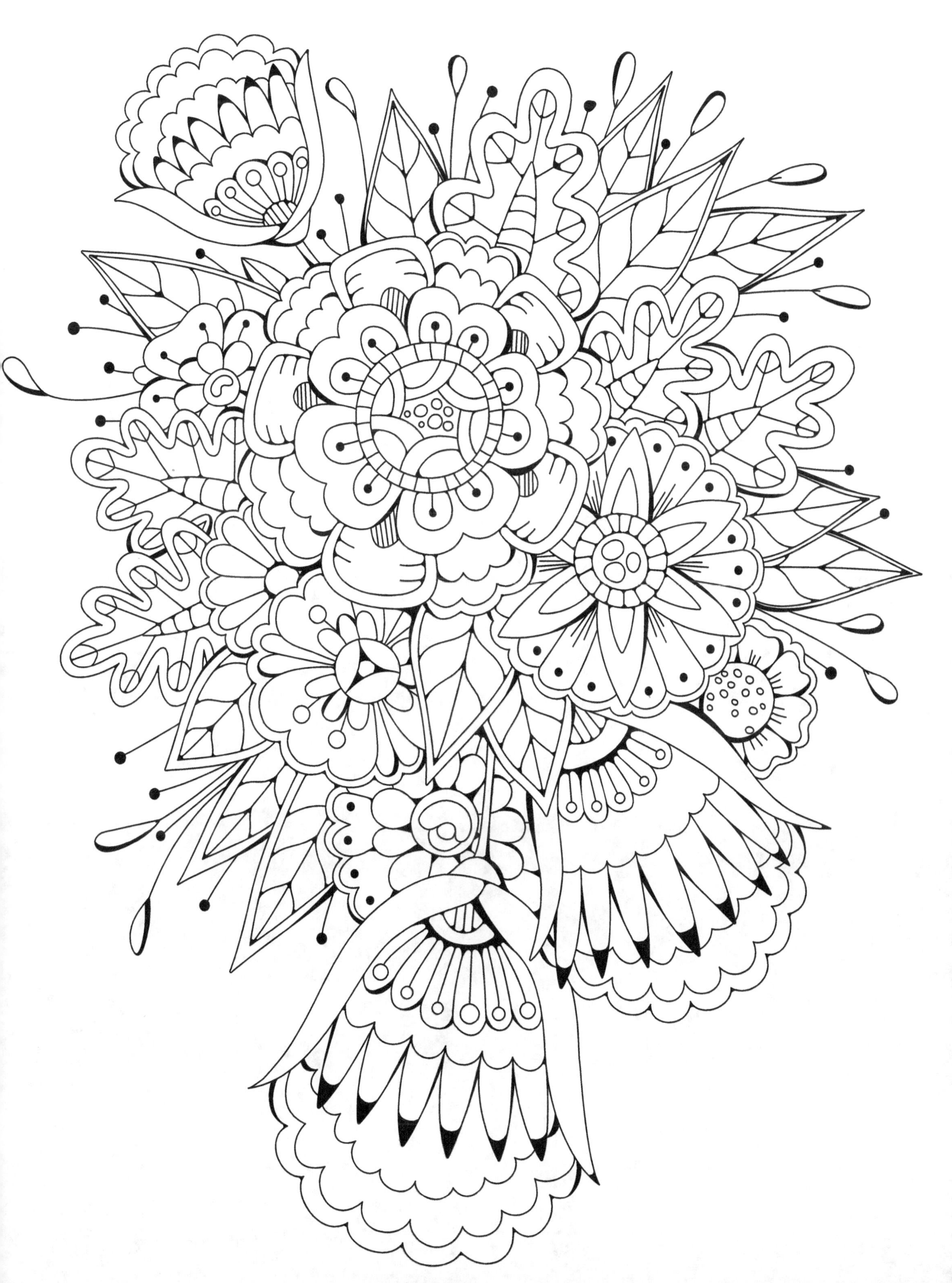

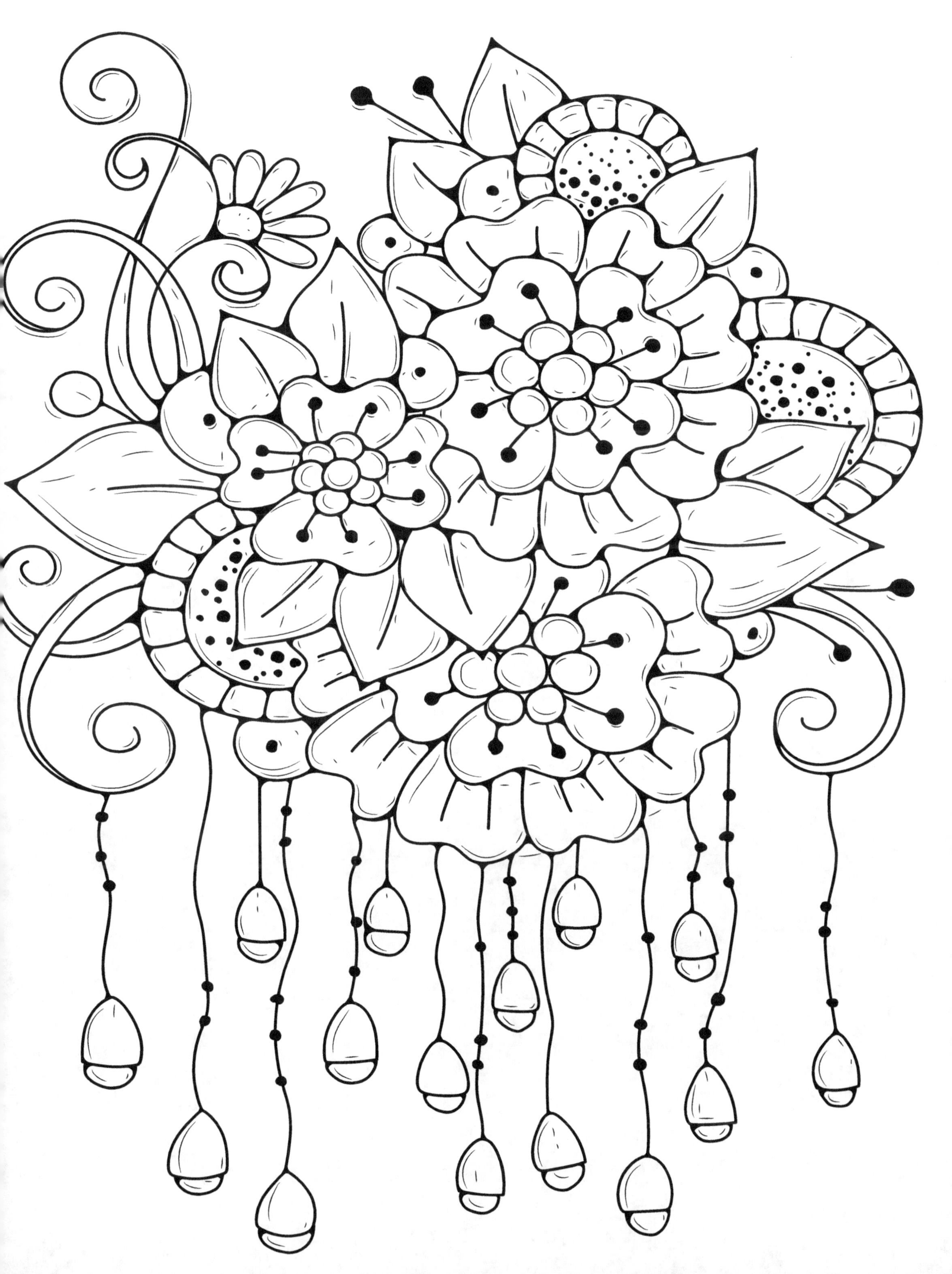

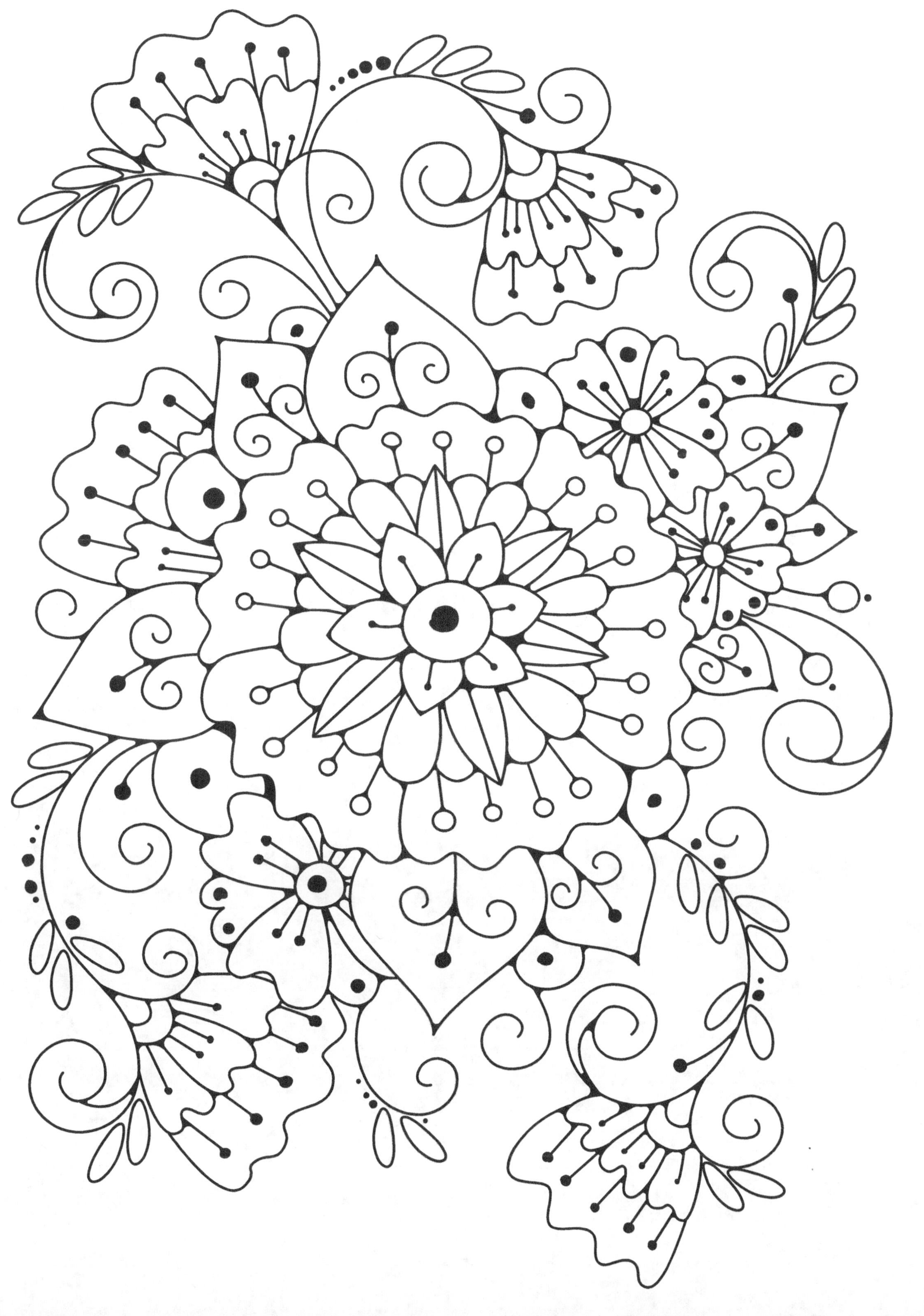

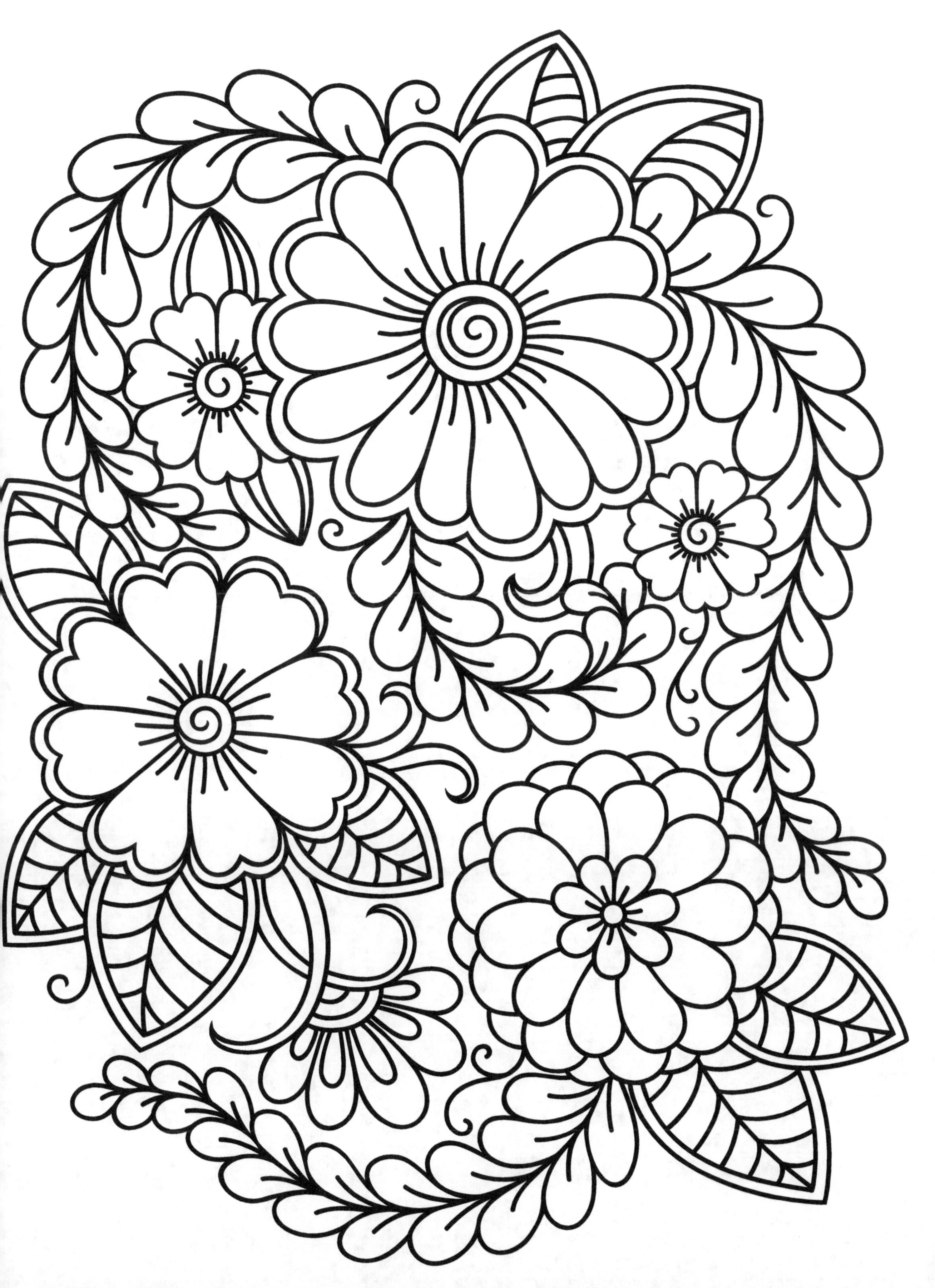

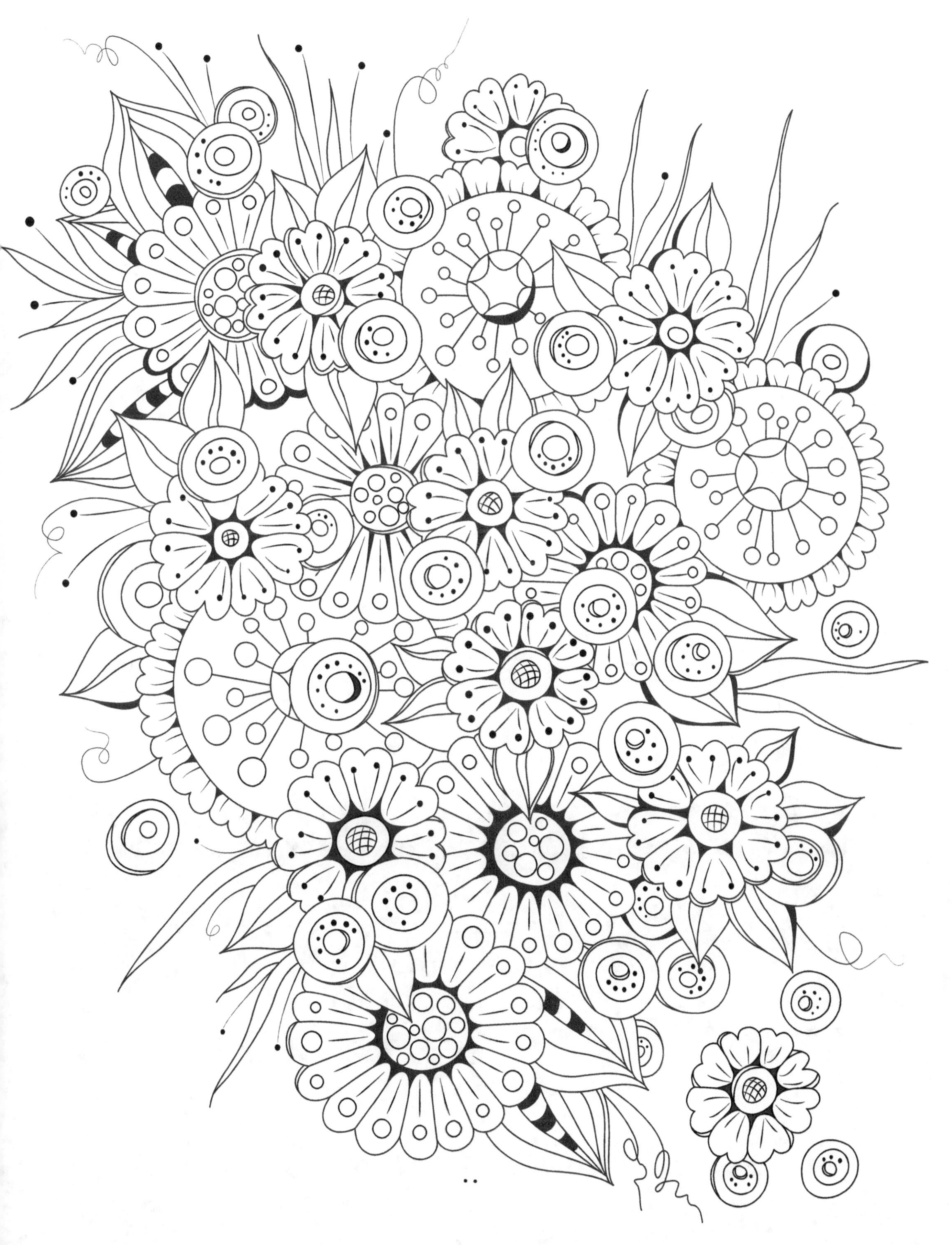

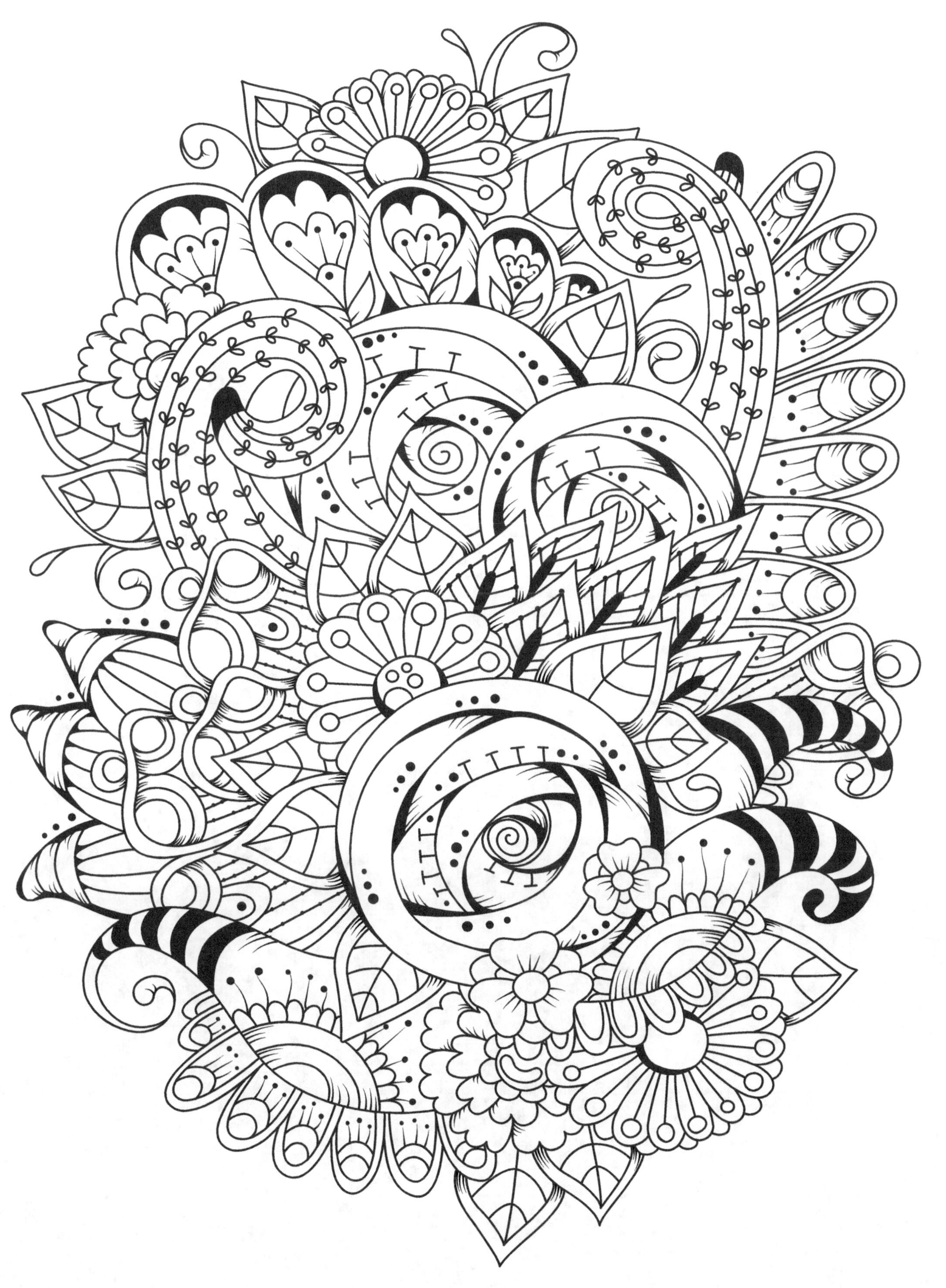

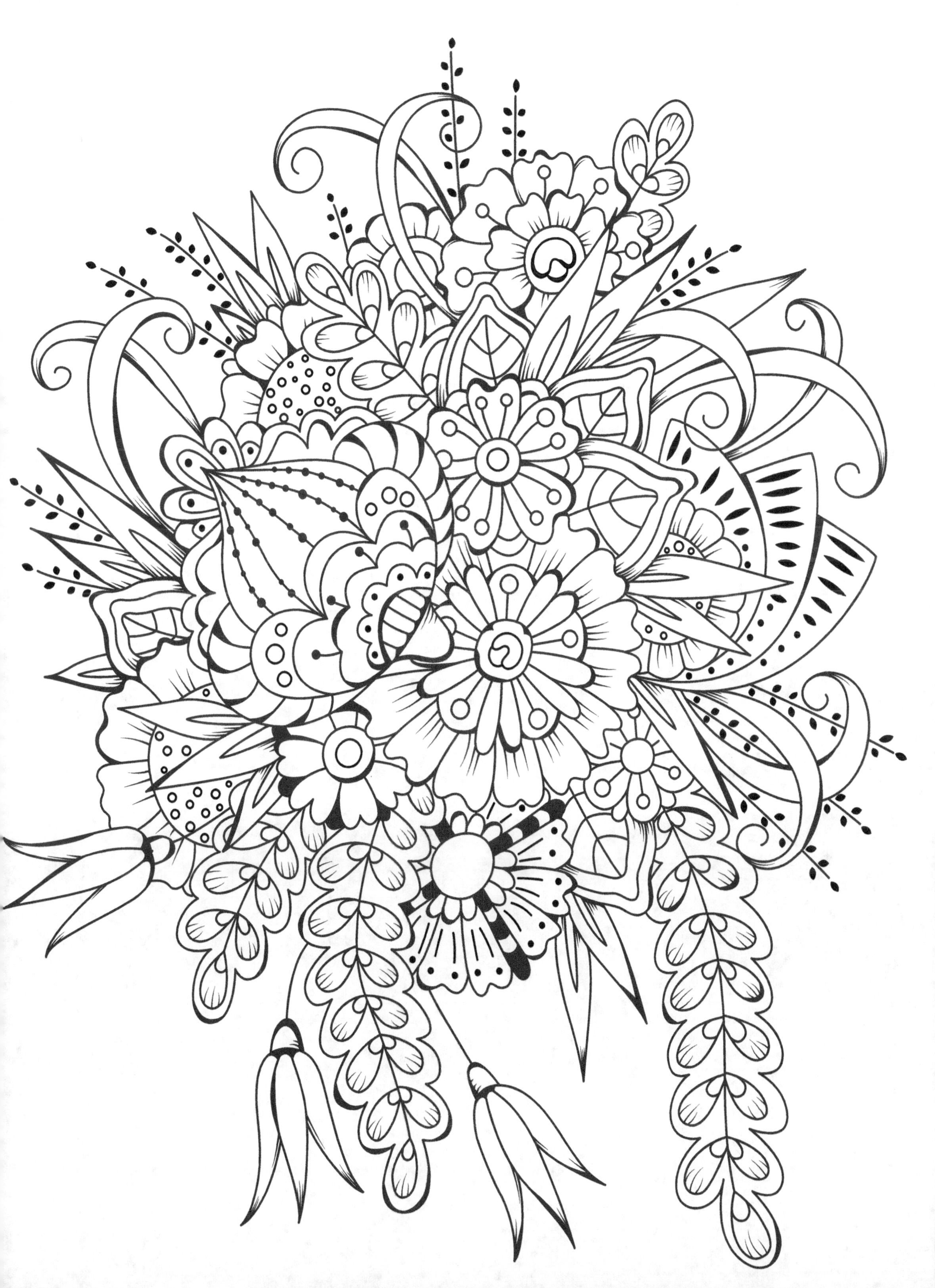

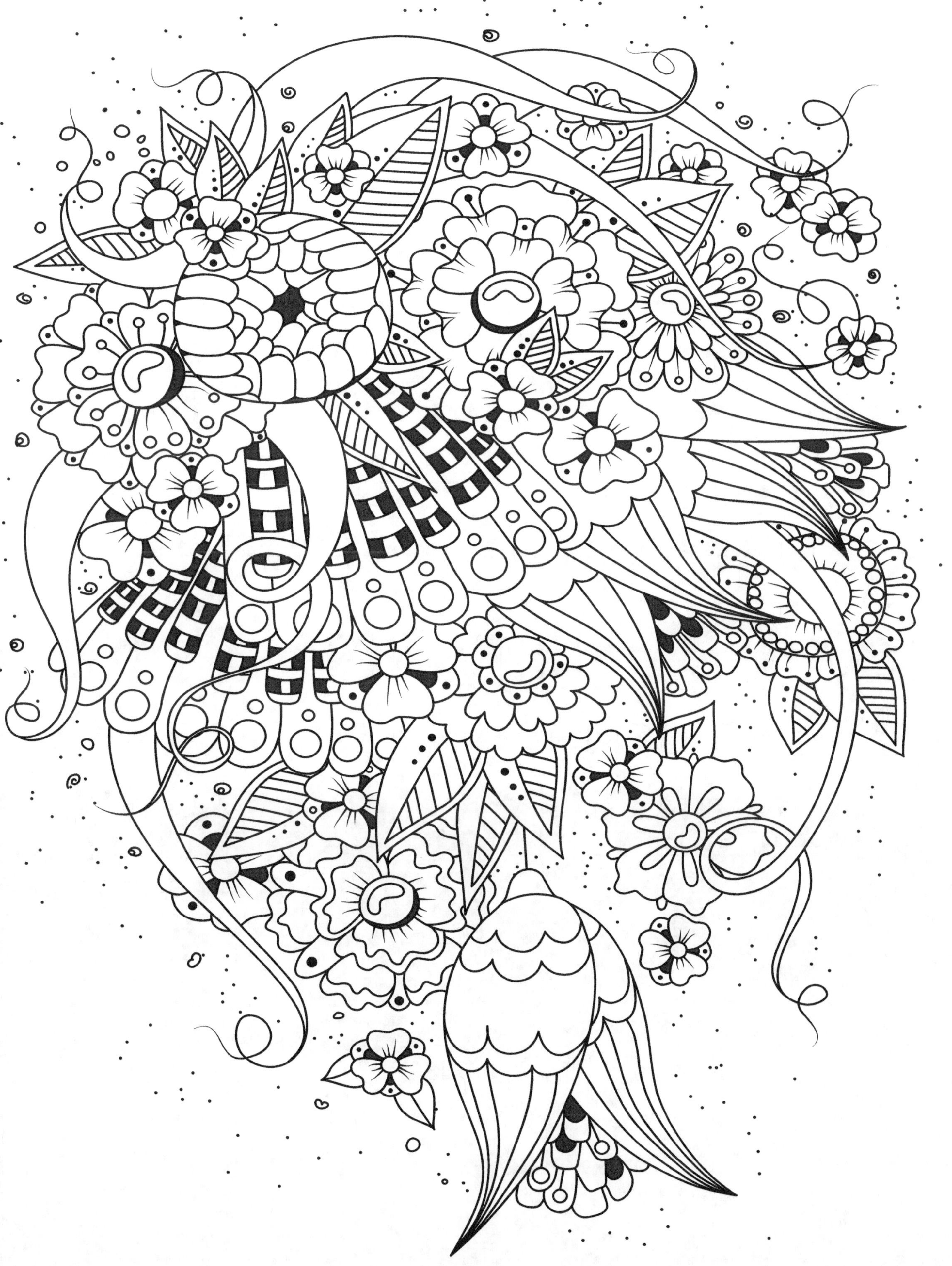

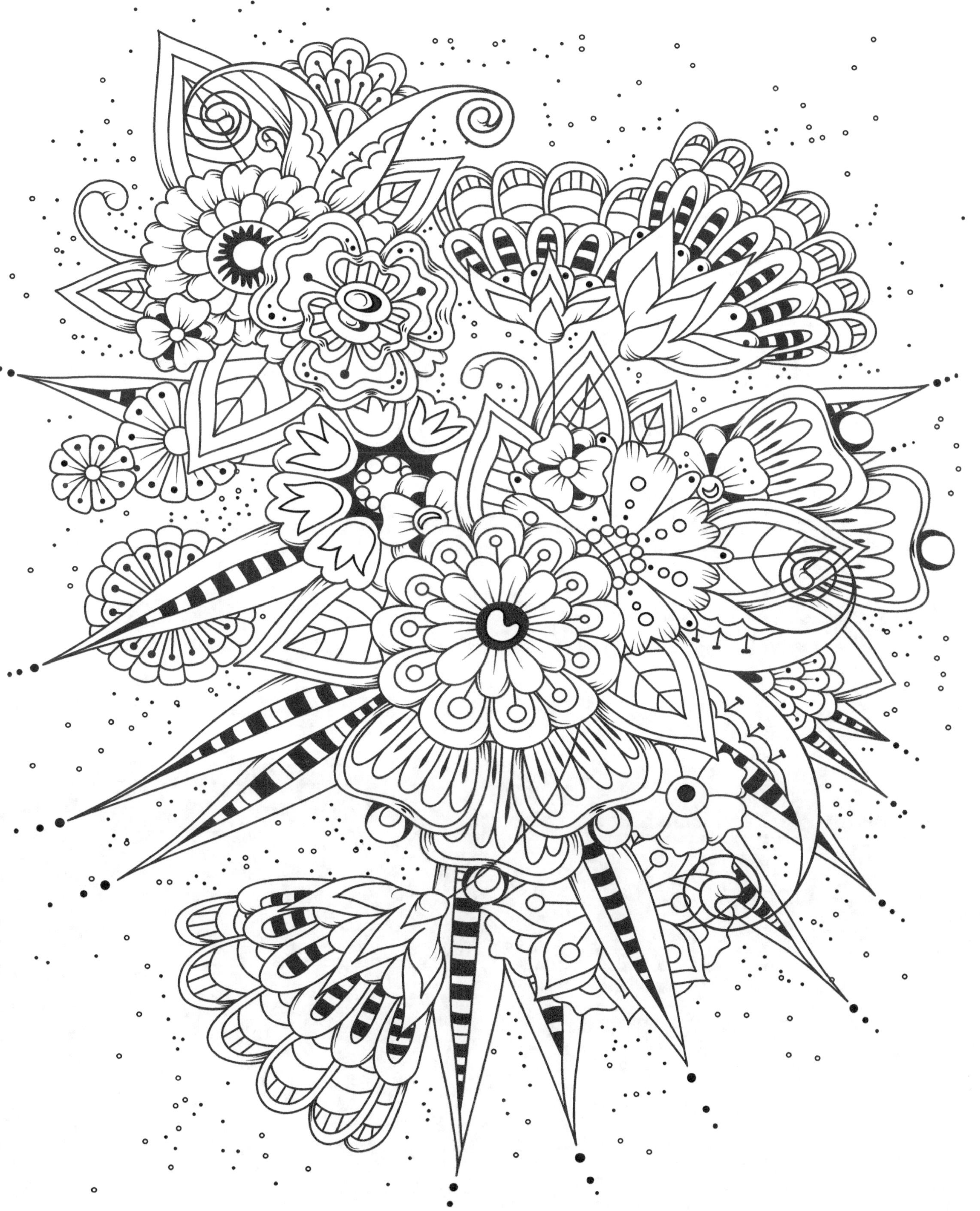

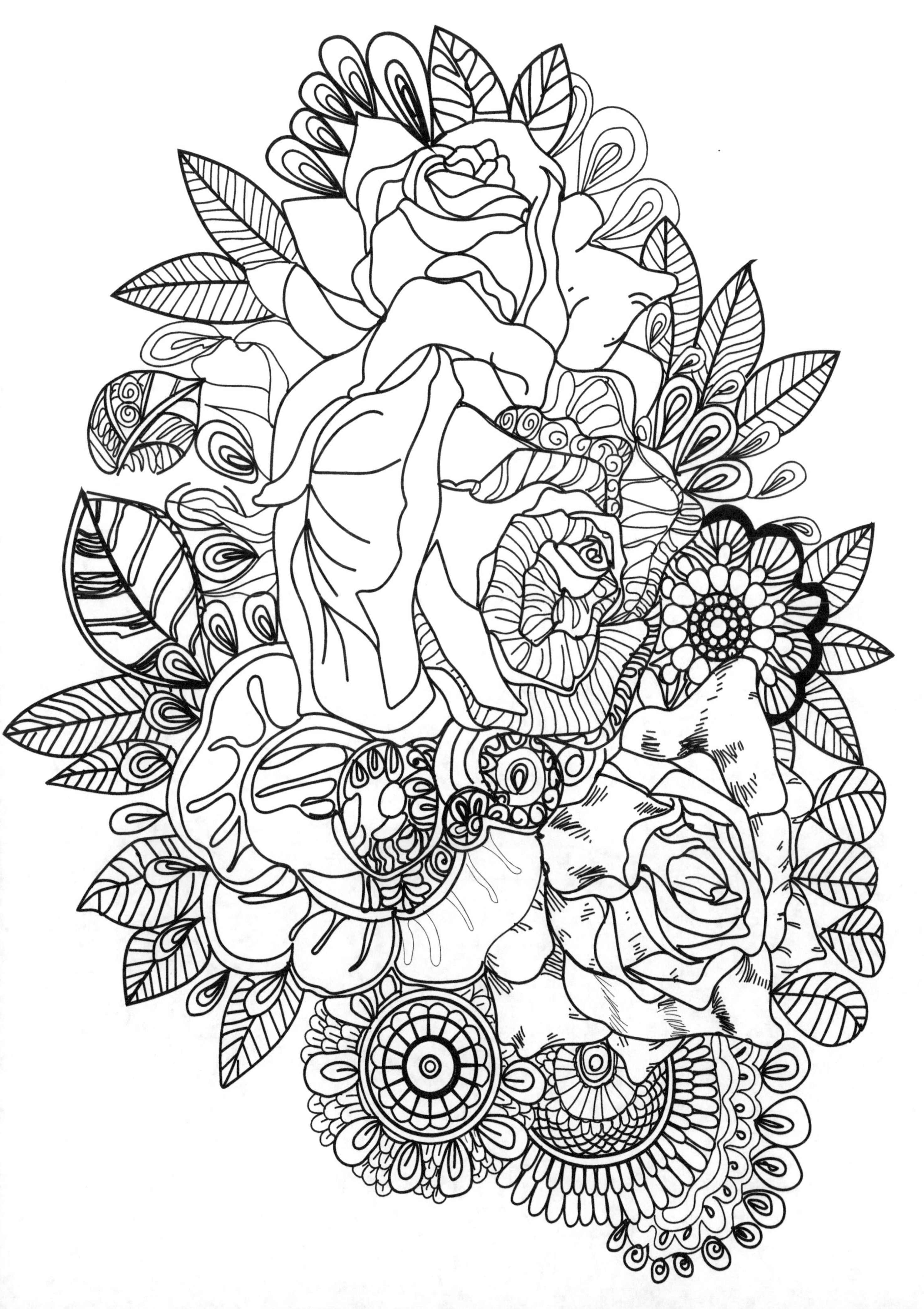

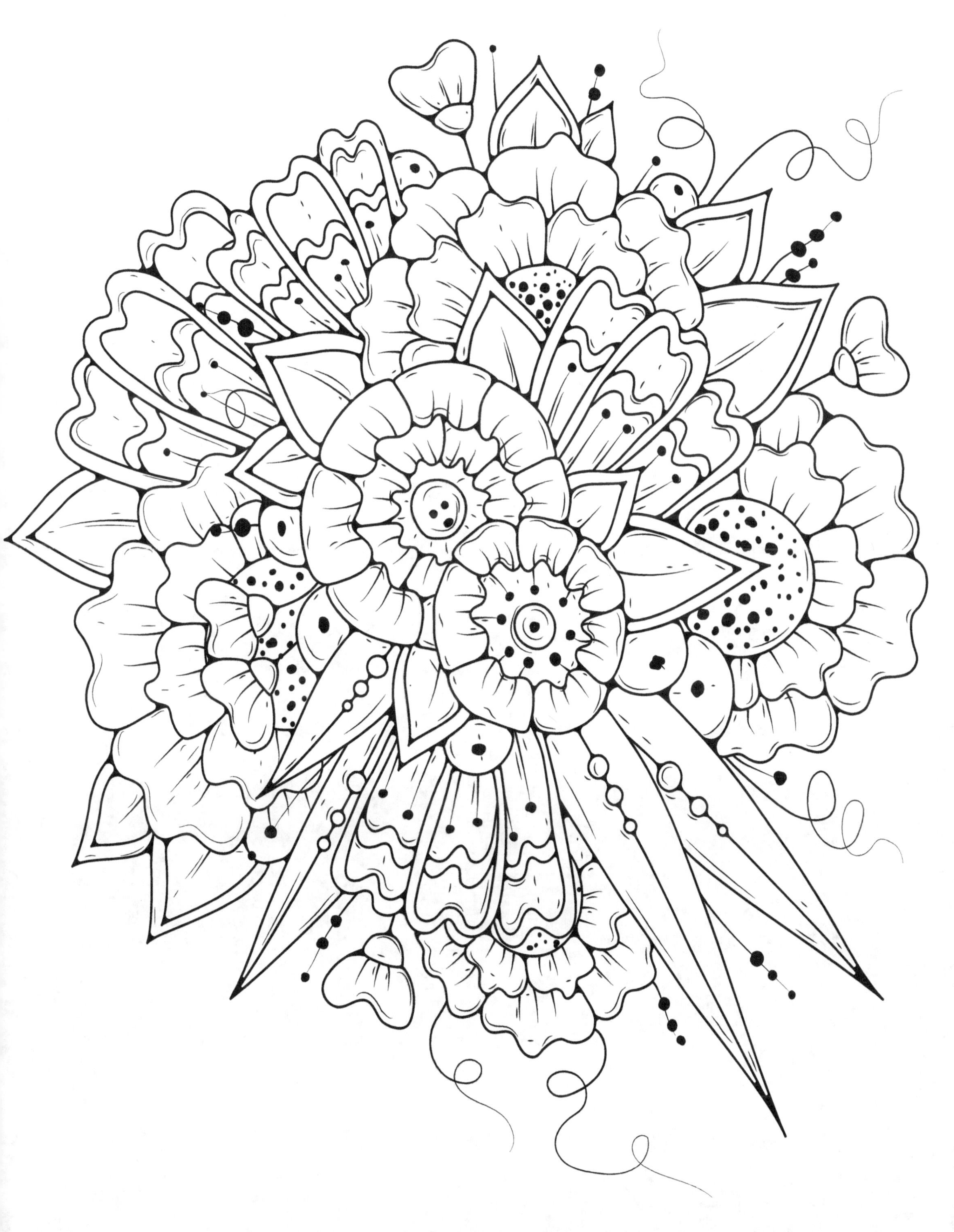

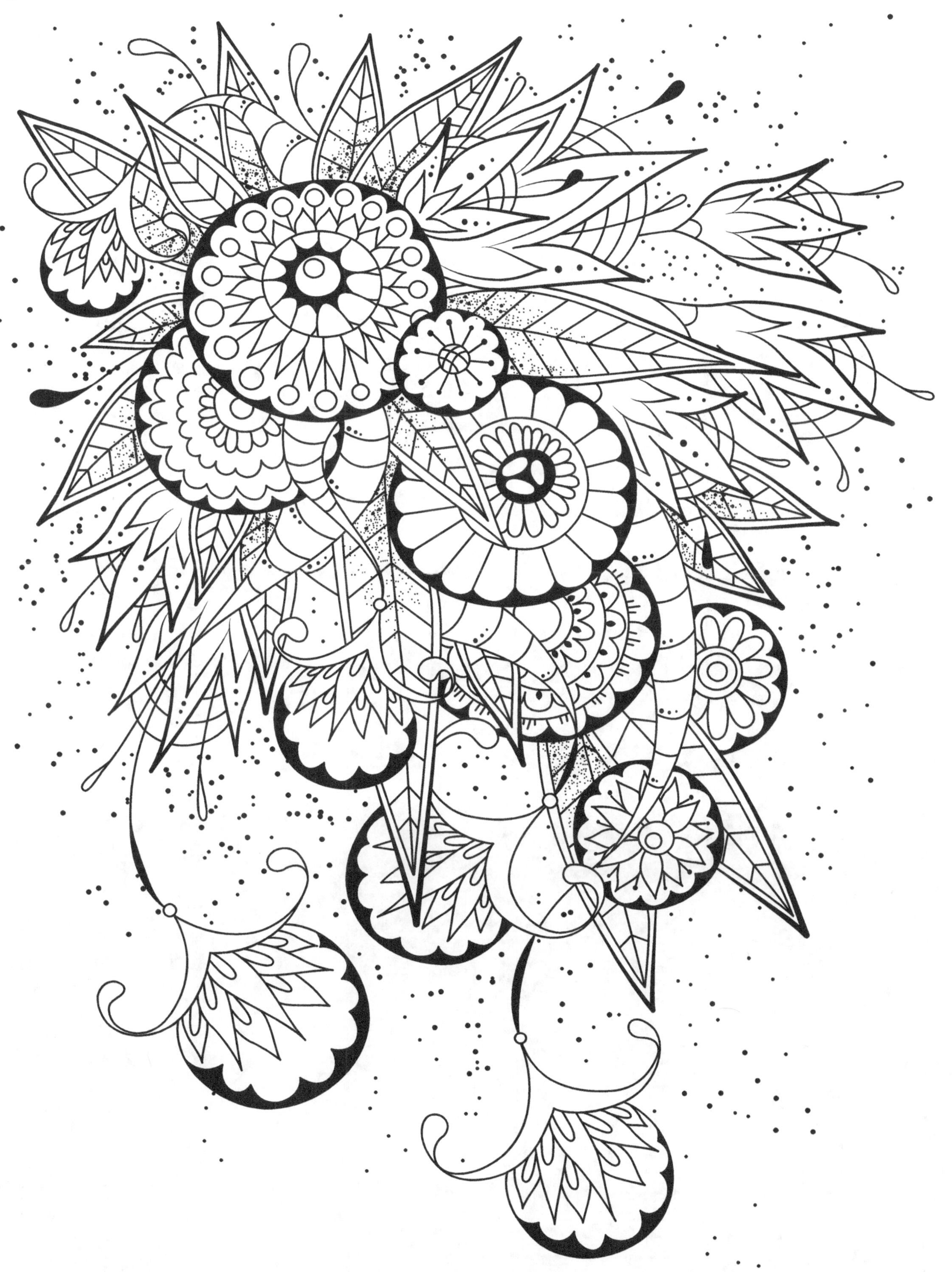

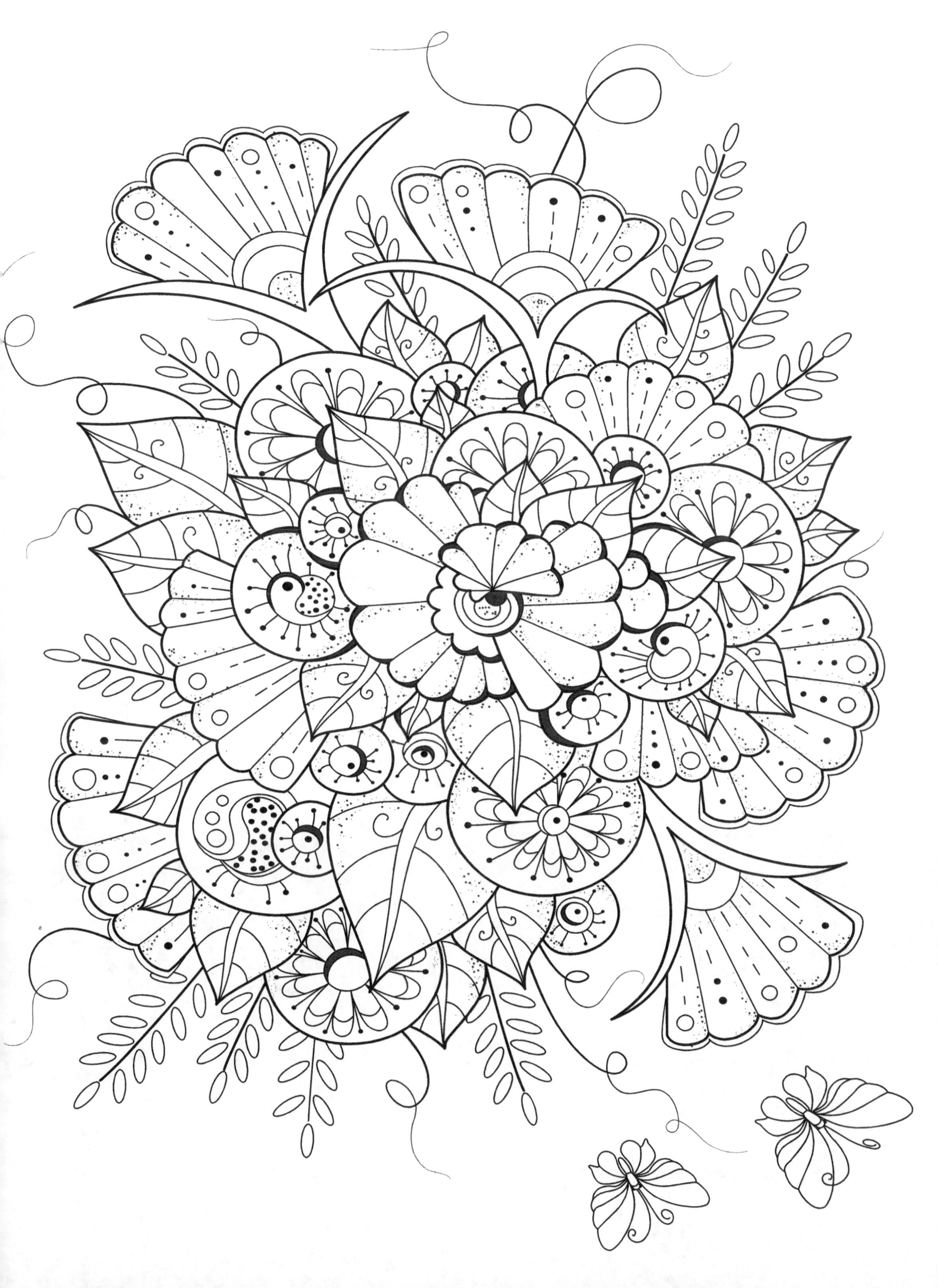

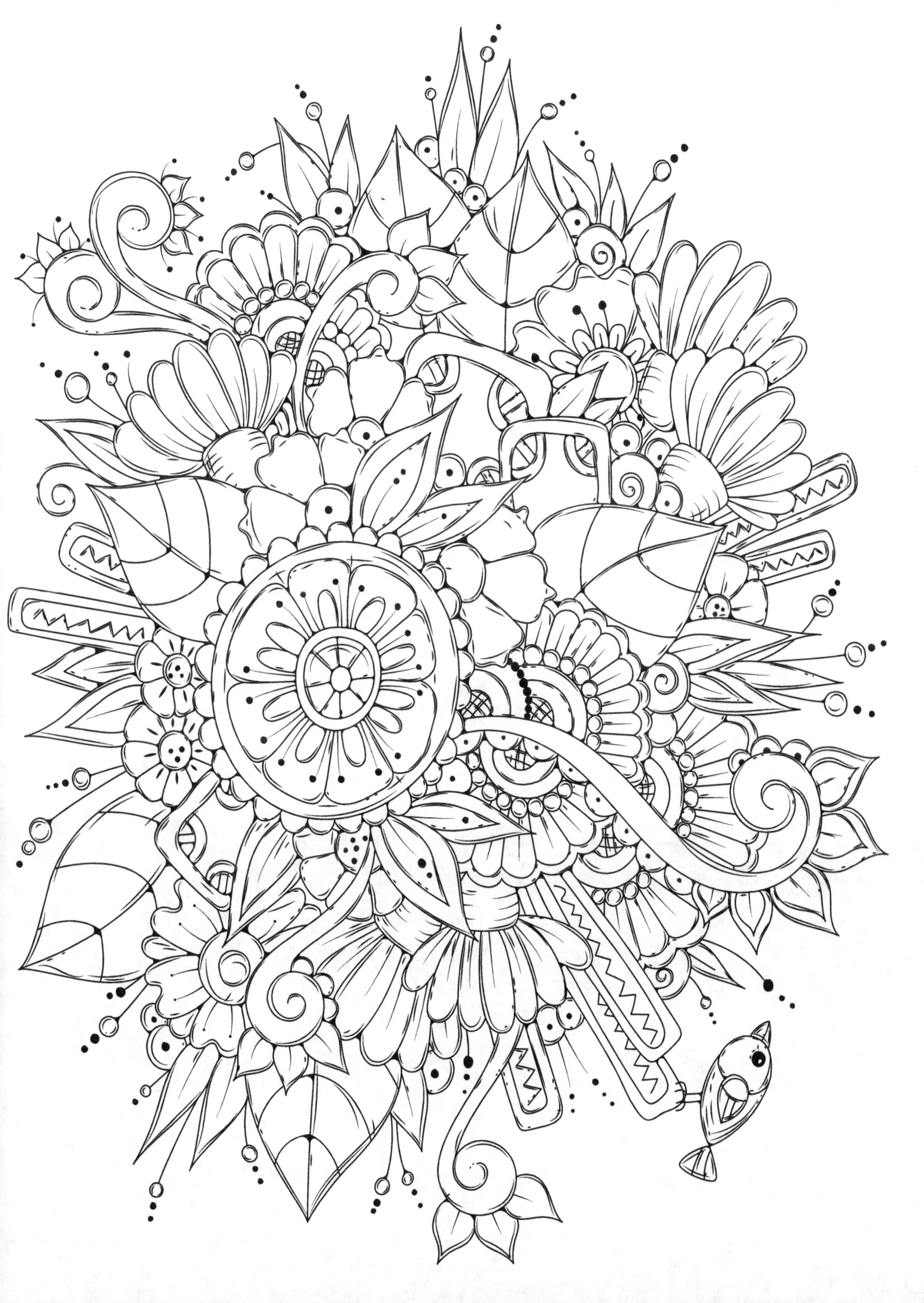

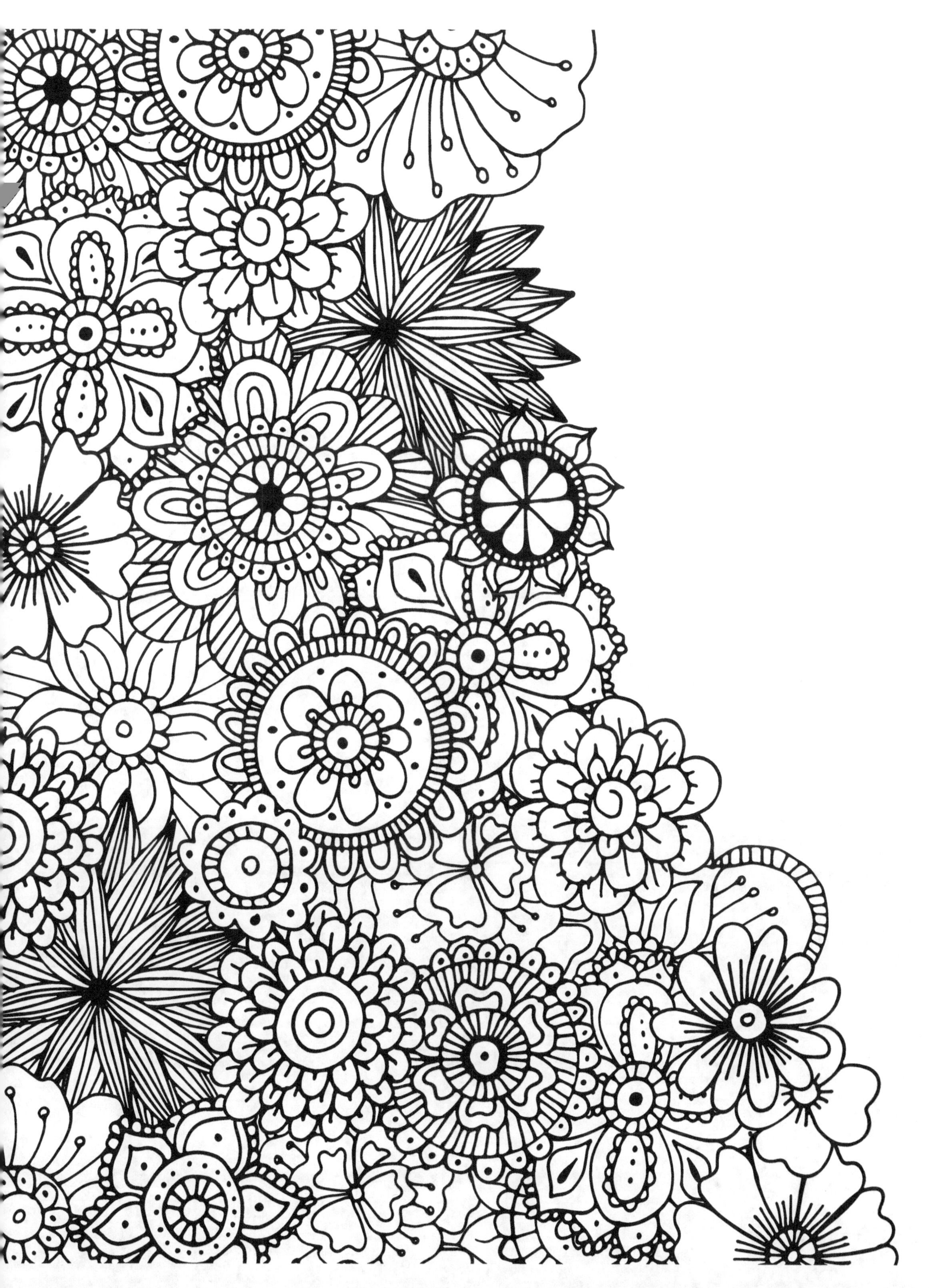

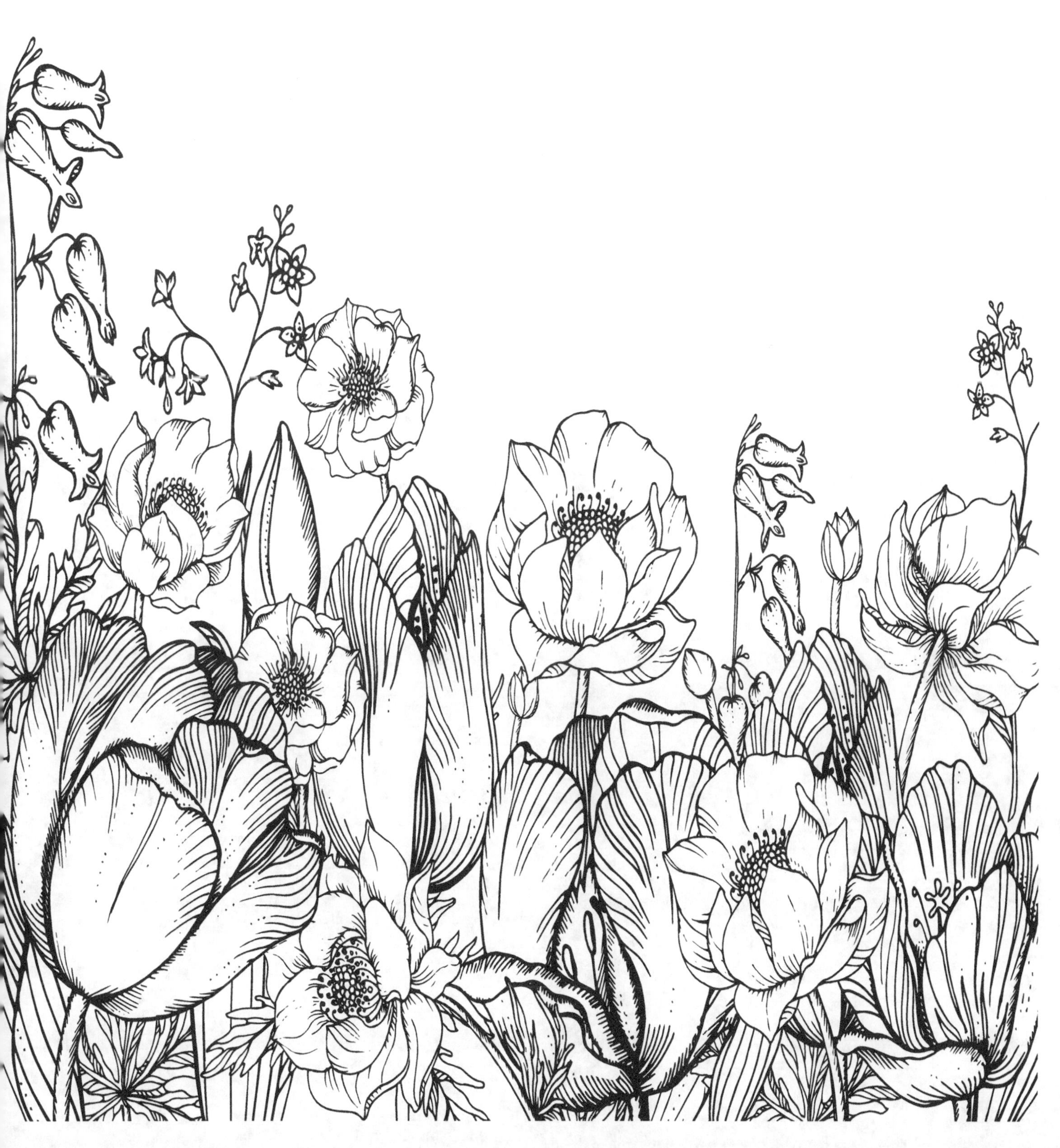

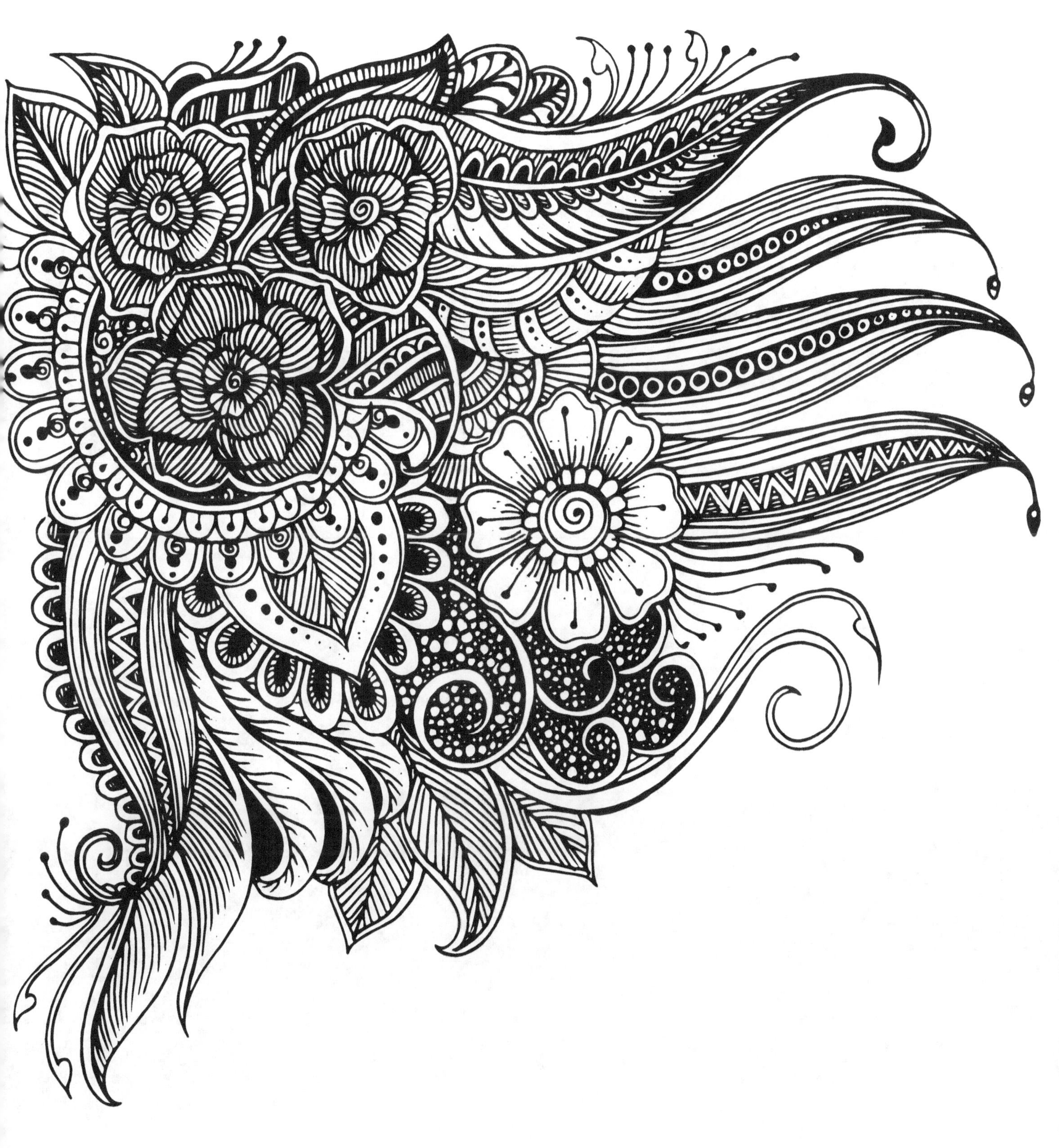

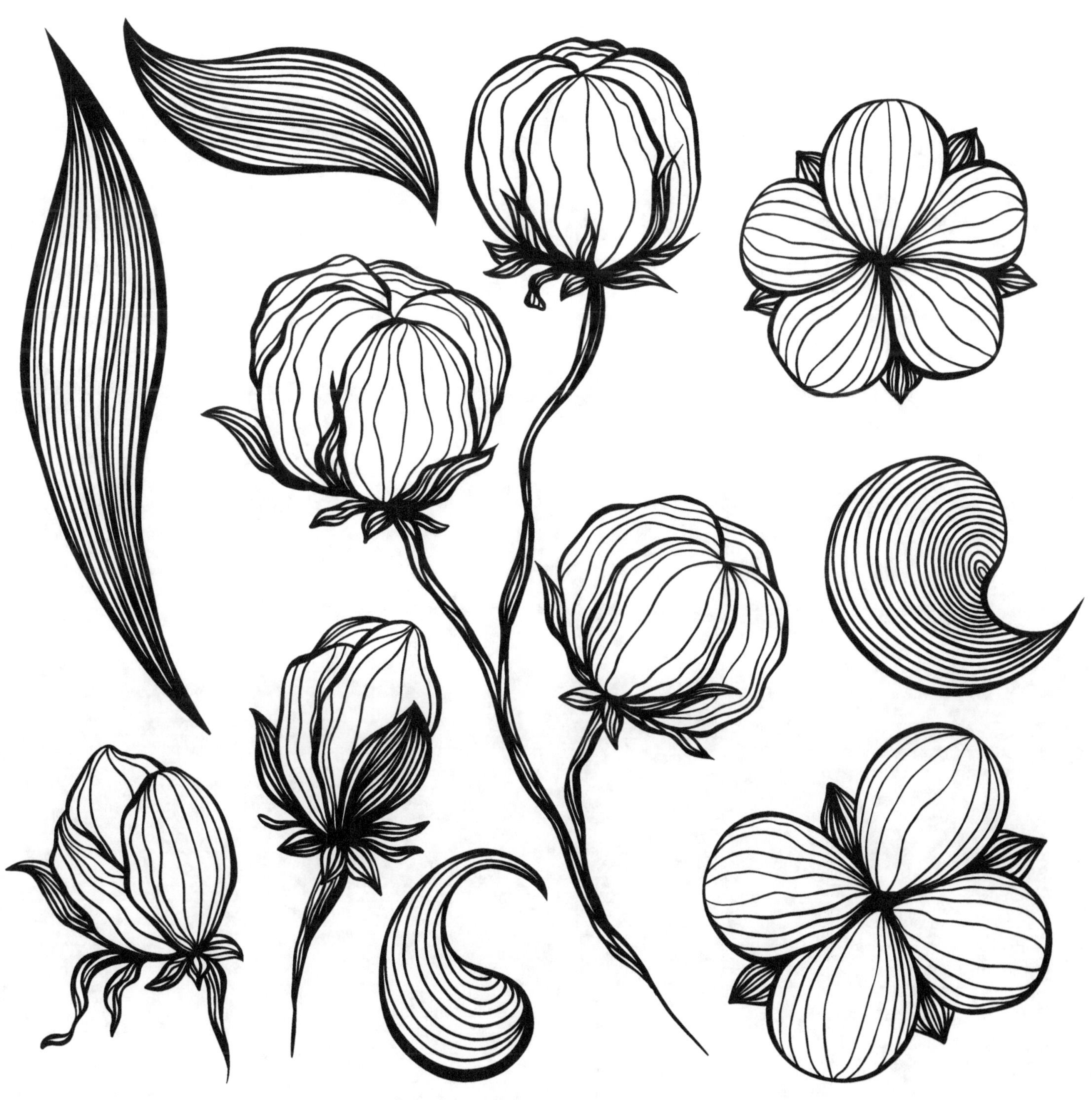

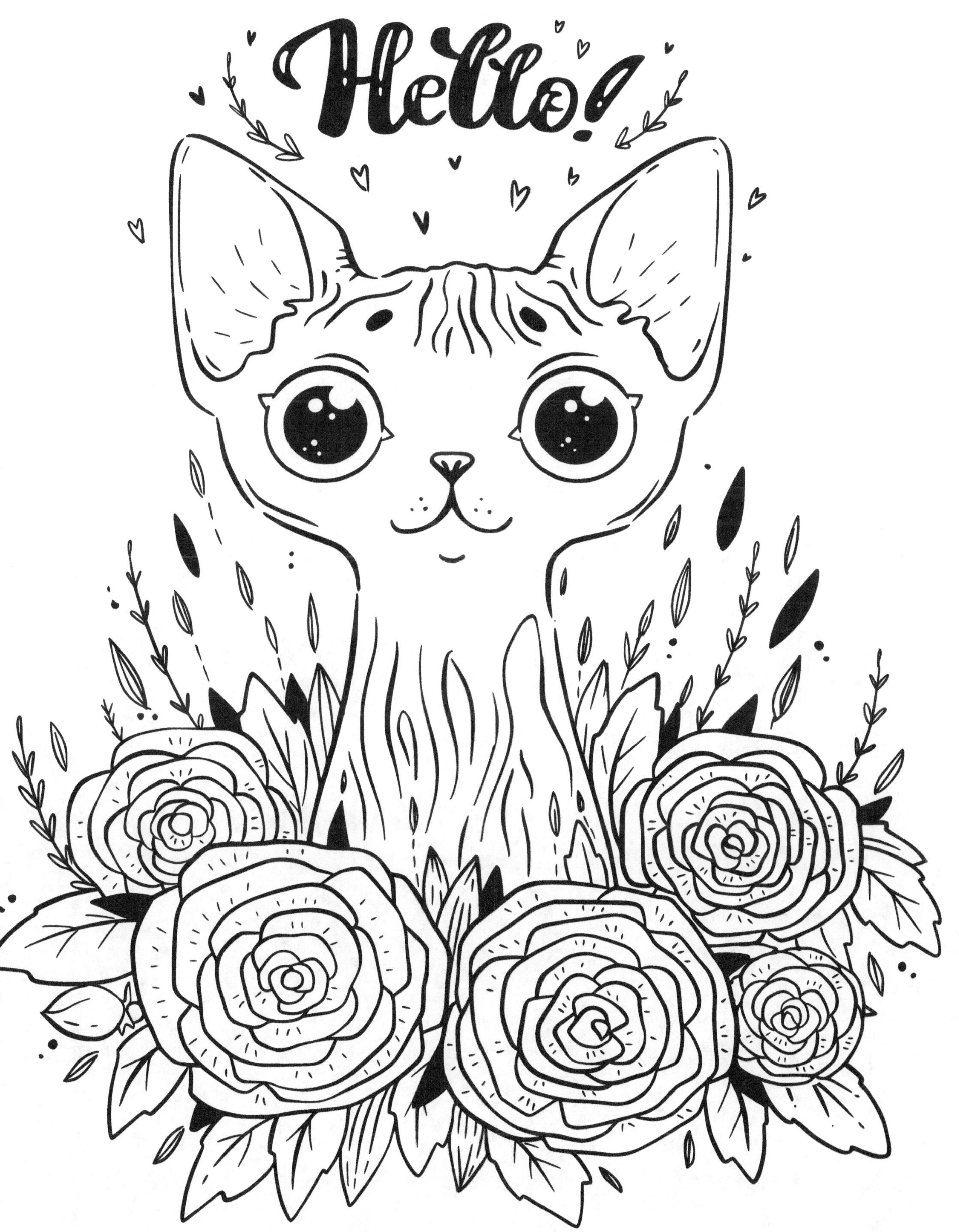
Hello!

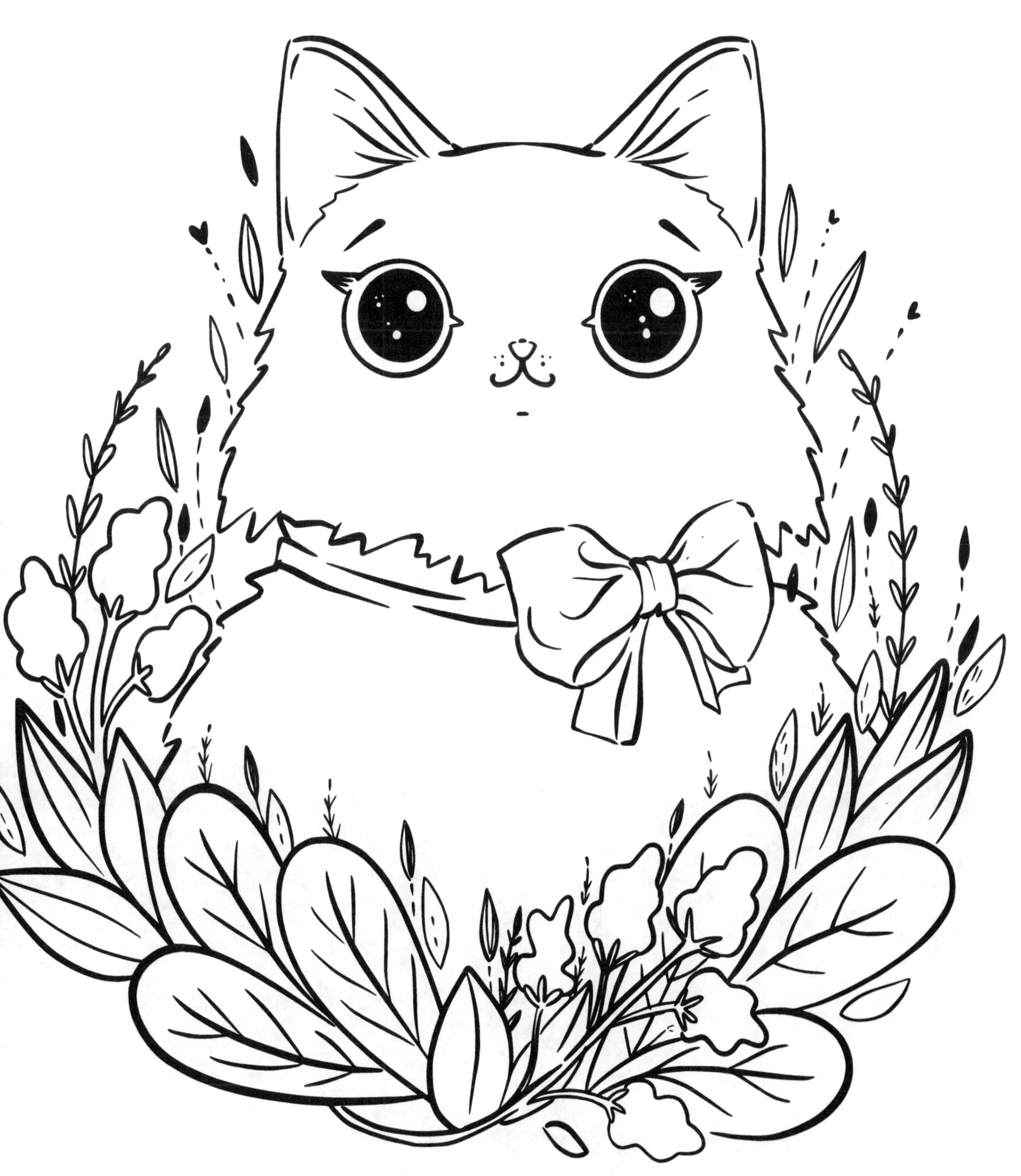

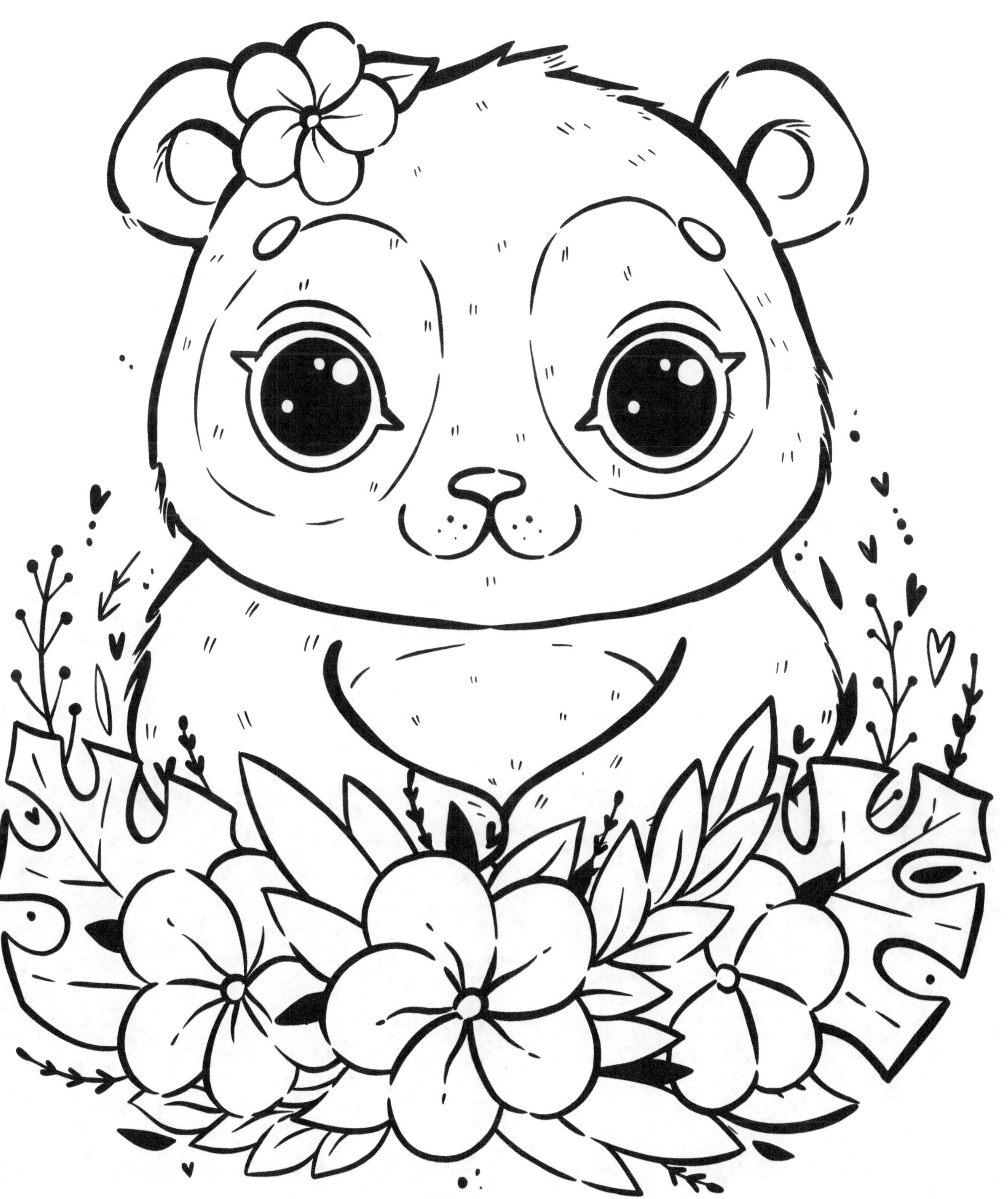

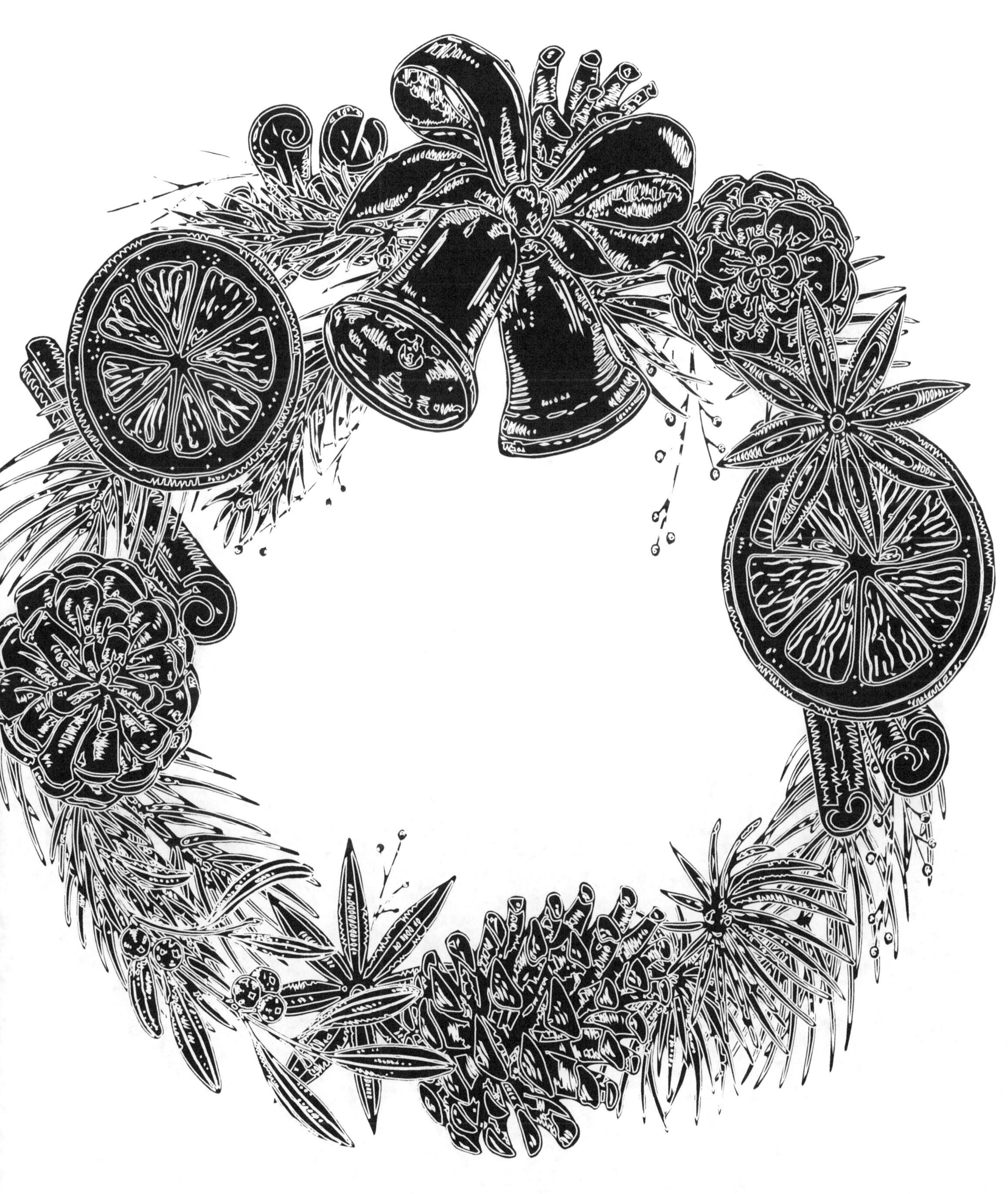

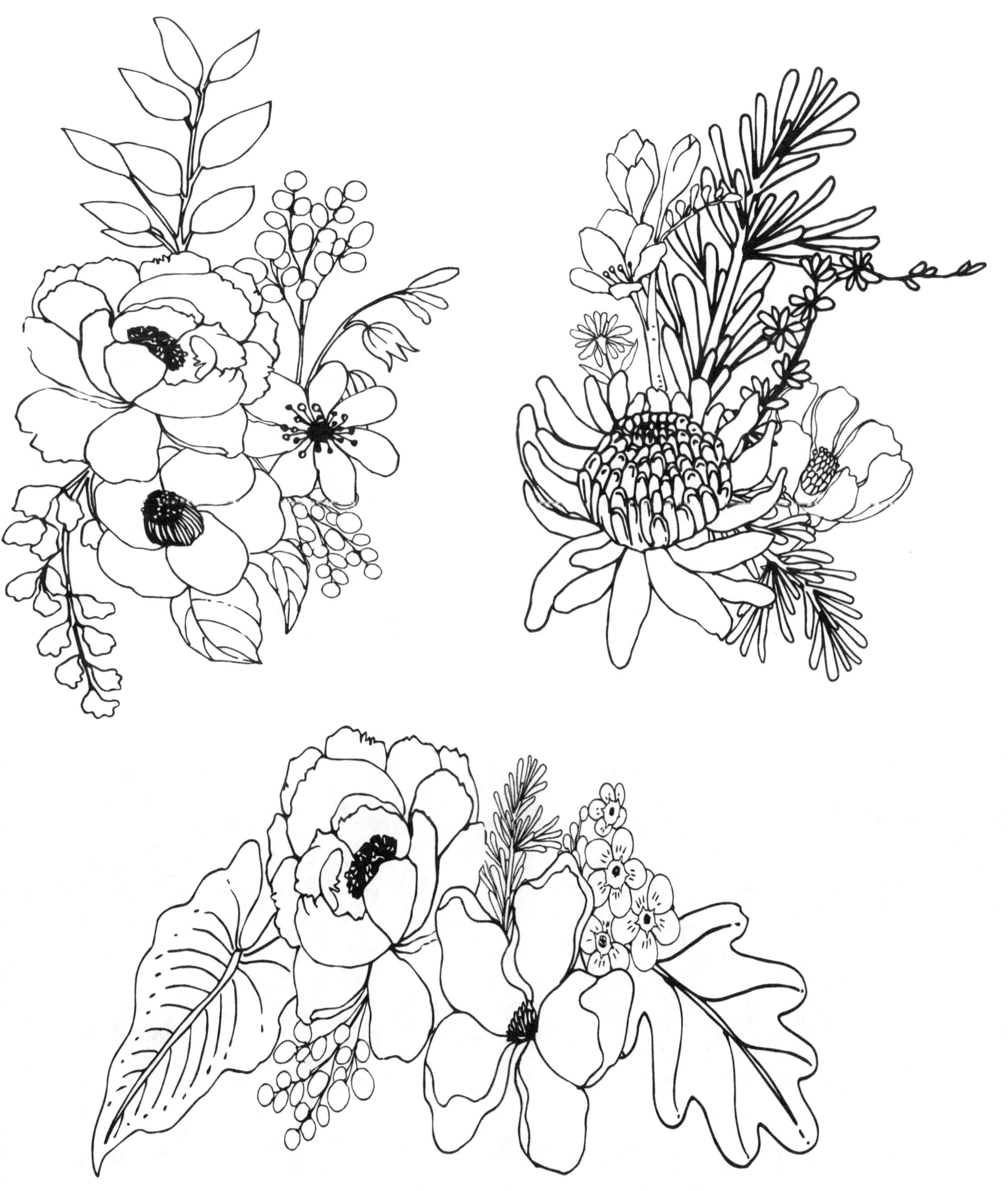

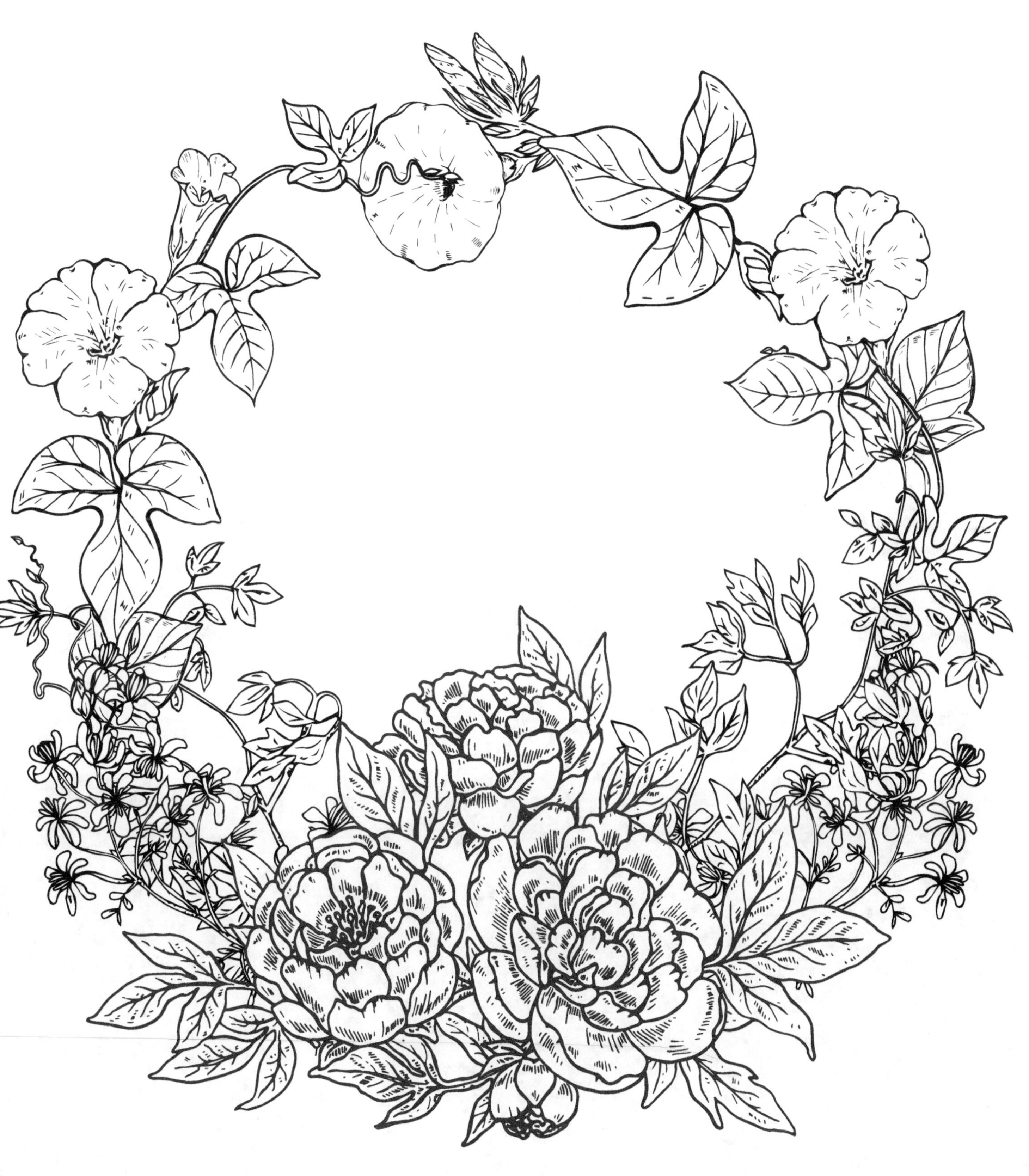